The Fugitive

A true and faithful account of the amazing experiences and eventual conversion of a Prussian deserter. Noted down from his own verbal relation and put in book form

by

J. DE LIEFDE

and translated in English by

MARCUS BANFIELD

ZOAR PUBLICATIONS
44 Queen's Drive, Ossett,
W. Yorks. WF5 0ND.

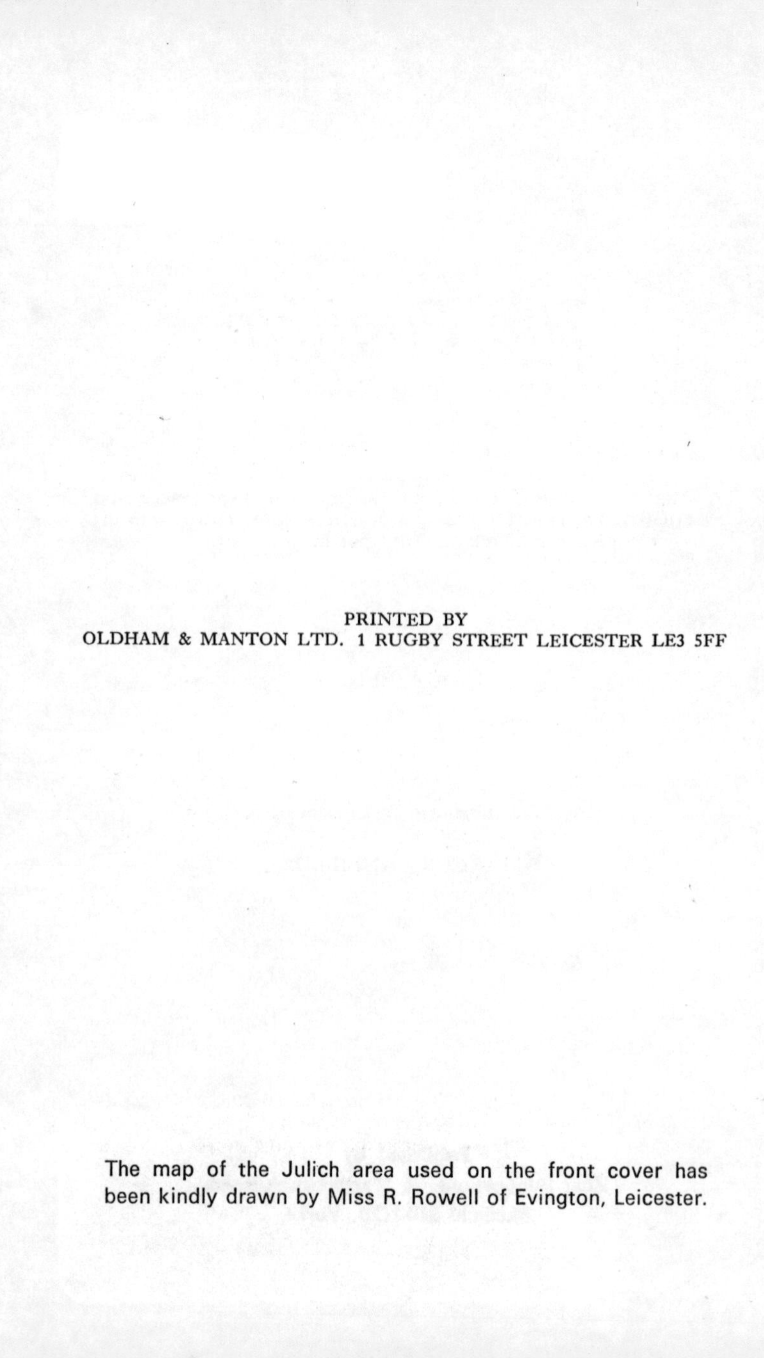

PRINTED BY
OLDHAM & MANTON LTD. 1 RUGBY STREET LEICESTER LE3 5FF

The map of the Julich area used on the front cover has been kindly drawn by Miss R. Rowell of Evington, Leicester.

PREFACE

When I was living in Elberfeld—it was in the year 1848—I paid a visit one evening to a friend who was one of the leading manufacturers of the city. Our conversation turned upon that important subject, the wonderful leadings of God in the conversion of a sinner.

"Yes," said my friend, "In this matter we often see that God's ways are not our ways, and that His thoughts are higher than our thoughts. Many a one of whom at first we may have had hopes, turns to a wicked way and dies with a curse on his lips; but many a one also, whom we are ready to imagine lost, is brought back by God in the most striking manner. Of this latter case I know of an instance at very close quarters, a more striking example than which I have seldom come across. I have among my factory workers one who may truly be put forward as an example of the power of divine grace. When you were with me in the factory just now you saw him standing by the largest boiler. Were this man to relate his story to us, he would be able to engage our attention for more than one evening."

"My dear friend, I pray you," said I, "could you by any means give me the opportunity of hearing his story?"

"Certainly, this very evening if you so desire."

"Very willingly; I have the time."

Without further ado, my friend had his employee called. Meanwhile I asked for writing materials, and very soon the factory worker entered the room. He was a man in the prime of life, not yet forty years old, and of a strong and handsome appearance.

"Baumfeller!" said my friend to him, "sit down and just gather your thoughts together. You must relate your experience to us and give to this gentleman the information which he requires."

"Sir," replies the workman in tolerably pure German, "there is nothing which I do more willingly; a relation of my history is nothing other than a tribute to the grace and long-suffering mercy of my God.

I do not therefore require to gather my thoughts; for however long I live I shall never be able to forget what God has done for me, and though I were to be wakened in the middle of the night, I would have everything as clearly in my mind's eye as though it happened but yesterday."

I sat down therefore and listened to the worker's story with my pen in hand. I have as far as possible taken down his words verbatim; but since I do not understand the worthy science of stenography or shorthand, it goes without saying, I have been obliged to note the workman's speech with many abbreviations. I have consequently in my notebook several pages full of half- and uncompleted words.

My readers would scarcely urge the love of truth so far as to insist that I should send these abbreviated notes to the press without any alteration whatever. I have in any case permitted myself the liberty of joining these bits and pieces into a coherent whole, by supplementing what was lacking in style and language to the best of my ability.

Neither have I deemed it necessary or profitable to retain the name of the workman, since he is still in the land of the living; but whoever is acquainted with him will guess without difficulty from the name Baumfeller, who the man is of whom we speak. With the exception however of these additions in style and language, it can be taken for certain that the story which now follows contains from beginning to ending complete veracity, and that no occurrence is there mentioned which has not actually taken place.

In guarantee whereof I set down my name without hesitation.

J. DE LIEFDE.

The Fugitive

I was born, began the workman, in the country town of Lennep, not far from Elberfeld, on the 18th February 1813. My father was a mill-worker, a wool-weaver who earned but a crust for me, my two brothers and my sister. In my early youth he moved to the town of Ronsdorf, where I obtained under the preacher Bruninkhaus, some introduction in religion. It was difficult for my father to earn enough to keep me and I had therefore to do mill work at a very tender age. Nonetheless I learned to read and write properly for I went willingly to school and my father well knew that without such knowledge I would make little progress in the world. In between times, while other boys played, I had to sit diligently at the spinning wheel and later at the loom. You can well imagine, sirs, that this was very much against my will, and there arose many a scene between my father and me, of which I cannot now think without praying with David; "Remember not the sins of my youth." My father soon knew not what to do with me and sent me to Lennep to work in a factory. This was more to my liking, apart from the fact that I had to hand over every single penny which I earned. I thought to myself: I will not stick at this for long, and as soon as there is an opportunity to change, I will run away.

My good father was a man who held before me the way of truth; for he was a faithful soul, who served God uprightly. But piety is not inherited; at least that was demonstrated in my case; for I put my father's gracious example to one side and preferred to turn to those things my eyes saw and hands touched. When then my father passed to his eternal rest in peace while I was still in Lennep, I realised that I was my own lord and master. I was seventeen and a sturdy, grown-up lad. It so happened that there was at that moment a shortage of work in the mill so that I had nothing to do. Lack of work was one thing which I hated with my whole heart, especially since my circumstances were such that shortage of hours was always accompanied by shortage of money. In brief then, I volunteered for service and became a rifleman in the fourth Rifle Brigade (Schutzenabteiling), in which I signed on for five years.

I was quite proud of my new soldier's uniform, and even more pleased with the happy soldier's life. It seemed indeed that I was a born soldier; for I became adept at manoeuvres, was always at my post, could drink enormously, had none to better me at cursing and was always happy and without a care. My officers were fond of me; for I took care that there should be nothing with which they would find fault, so that during the whole five years' service I was not once arrested. My comrades were fond of my company, for at my front door was mirth and at my back door was pleasure.

2

Thus five years flew by. We were stationed in Aachen and I had but ten days to go. Then my time would be up. It was the 1st January 1835 when I went with about twenty of my comrades in the evening to the public-house, in order for once to drink the New Year in right joyfully. There was drinking, dancing and playing in abundance, a life of abandon, in which all the cares and troubles of life became lost in forgetfulness. At the New Year I gave no more heed to the transitory nature of time, than to cry out with glass in hand: "Let us eat, drink and be merry, for tomorrow we die!" Such is the condition of the heart of a man who knows not God and cares not for his own soul. With a curse upon his lips and the drunkard's glass in his hand, he rushes laughing to meet the eternal and dreadful judgment of God.

It was eight o'clock and the tattoo was sounded, close enough to be heard, for the "pub" was right opposite the main guard-house. But I had ears only for the violin, and as little cared for the tattoo as for the eternal welfare of my soul. A military policeman arrives and asks those present to show their passes to prove that they had received permission to be absent from the tattoo. When he came to me, I said with an oath: "Go to—with your pass! I have not got one!"

"Then I must arrest you and take you to the guard house." With these words he placed himself behind me and ordered me to march before him. I refused, for I was intoxicated and cared for neither rules nor laws. My comrades surrounded me and the policeman and there arose an almost hellish clamour. Meanwhile the policeman called the guard and I soon found myself in the guard-room. Even there I was not quiet however. I tried to escape through one of the two doors, but was held fast by two comrades with whom I now began to struggle. At this moment, the lieutenant whose round it was, came in, and seeing me acting so wildly, shouted various curses at me, commanded me to be still, threatened me with his fist and punched me twice upon my breast.

"Lieutenant!" I cried furiously, "Don't you touch me; you have hit me twice—but there will be no third time!"

Scarcely were these words out of my lips when he struck me for the third time. I sprang forward, threw him to the ground and gripped him by the throat. The soldiers rushed forward at once, dragged me by main force away from him and brought me without further delay to the detention room.

Once there in the silent cell, I fell asleep and slept out my drunken fit. On awaking the following morning I recollected with a start what had taken place. I knew the law and realised that death was the sentence for my offence. When this became clear to me, my soul was overcome with dismay. I spent the whole day in the most terrible apprehension, yes almost in despair. Methinks I then experienced in some measure what the condemned shall feel in hell. I tore out my hair and cast myself upon the ground. Once and again a few of my gracious father's words or some Bible texts came into my mind, but they fell upon my soul like hailstones upon a slate roof. Nowhere could I find comfort; I saw my young life suddenly cut off in the midst of pleasure by death. I gave little thought to eternity, but much to my present misery. I was completely disconsolate.

The third day I was brought before the court-martial and indeed condemned to death. The judges pitied me, the more so because I was esteemed in the Corps. I was counselled to appeal to the king for pardon. It was then that I experienced what consolation is afforded to a poor death-condemned man even if only in the possibility of receiving a royal pardon. I awaited the answer from Berlin in a state of alternating hope and fear. At last this answer came. The king had mitigated my sentence to one of twenty years hard labour.

On the 1st April 1835 I was transferred to the fortress of Julich, which is as you know on the road between Cologne and Dusseldorf. There I should spend the best part of my youthful days—twenty years—as one entombed, as one buried alive. How terrible to contemplate. Yet it was comforting when compared with the thought of death itself.

The life of a military prisoner in Julich is a most frightful one. The citadel in which the punishment block is situated, is built immediately against the town and is well secured. Entering a tremendous gate you cross a bridge. This leads you to a one hundred and fifty foot long "porterne", which is a vaulted passage in the rampart, above which men can walk, so to speak, over your head. Within this passage it is pitch dark. Passing through it, you come to a square; on your right you see the other rampart, and beside it the great barrack prison for offenders. This prison adjoins the great wall of the citadel and is built so low in the ground that, though it is of three storeys, its roof comes level with the footpath of the main rampart. There is no possibility of escape from it. Furthermore, the whole citadel is undermined to such an extent that one can get lost in the tunnels and passages. In a word, it is a place of terror. And there I should spend twenty years in hard labour!

In hard labour! Yes, for a condemned soldier life there is miserable in the extreme. I was placed in a room on the second floor, which accommodated 12 persons. The furniture is quickly described. There is a sink for the dirty water, two rough wooden tables and twelve wooden stools without backs. Besides this, there are two stoves, upon which the prisoners must heat their soup and coffee in the evening. Finally, each has a bed on which to sleep. That is all, there is nothing else to be seen.

3

And now for the life itself! In summer we had to be ready at four o'clock in the morning and could breakfast on a piece of dry bread, always provided that we had it; for each man obtained 3 kilogrammes of bread every three days. For me, at least, many a morning was commenced without breakfast. Parade was at a quarter past four, and woe betide us if our shoes did not gleam and our miserable kit was not carefully brushed! Thereupon each one was set to work, which consisted chiefly in digging, excavating, tree-felling, carrying produce, pushing wheelbarrows and other such heavy labours, which caused the sweat to stream down our bodies, and to me it was often better to die than to live. We worked at all times under the supervision of soldiers who guarded us with loaded rifles and were known as patrols. Having worked until 8 o'clock we were granted a half hour's rest before working on until 11 o'clock. We then returned to the citadel. Upon entering we were carefully searched for food, knives, files, or any other forbidden items.

We then proceeded to the kitchen, which was built against the prison-block, where each man collected his ration. This was a quantity which was really too small to live upon and yet too great to cause starvation. With this meagre portion, which normally consisted of some type of meal, each man received a measure of fat. We never saw meat, except on Sundays, when each man had a small portion. The result of this was that we all heartily longed for the Sunday, though alas! more for its carnal advantages than its spiritual. For the rest we received daily a measure of coffee, from which we drank four times, since we dried out the grounds again and again upon the stove and mixed it again with a little chicory. This chicory we had to buy from our own money; for we were paid 6 pennings per day, out of which we had to purchase washing materials, boot polish, hob-nails, thread and any other necessities for our cleanliness. You can well imagine, gentlemen, that we could not do much therewith; for tobacco alone 7 pennings were needed. It is therefore not surprising that stealing was commonplace, and there was an inexhaustible search for ways and means of smuggling items from the town through the compassion of the inhabitants.

As soon as each man had his ration, the room-mates went together to their cell. Once there the meal was commenced with the accompaniment of loud shouting and cursing. Without one prayer for blessing or even of thanks, we gulped it down like ravenous wolves. I experienced then however the powerful effect of upbringing. At home with my parents we had always said grace before and after meals, and though I feared not God, yet I could not accept that we should throw ourselves upon our food now like the beasts. So strong was my conviction in this that I withdrew with my bowl in order to partake of its contents in seclusion by my bed.

By 12 o'clock our meal had to be finished, the room cleaned and our share of the potatoes for the following day to be peeled. There followed another parade, and then work until 4 o'clock. After half an hour's rest we continued our labours until 6 o'clock, and then we returned to the barracks. We now had nothing more to eat or drink, apart from what we may have saved from the day's rations. Then at last began the most terrible part of this terrible life. Then, left to ourselves in our rooms we gave vent to the rancour which boiled within all our hearts. During my service I had heard many a malediction and witnessed many a scene; but such oaths and such outbursts of devilish fury as those I heard here, were beyond my imagination. Neither was there one spark of love to be traced in this world. The law governed here in all her terror. Among the lower ranked officers who had direct supervision of us, there was neither ghost nor shadow of mercy; they really were brutes and tyrants. At the slightest provocation 25 strokes were administered with a rod, the end of which was bound with wire. The victim of such a punishment would have a shoulder swollen to twice its normal size in consequence of the blood clotting. It was not uncommon for death to follow such a beating, and I have stood beside more than one dying prisoner who said with his last breath: "I owe this to the Prussian stick."

Another punishment was known as the "latten", or "the laths", this was indeed a tormenting machine. The culprit was placed in a square shed. The floor of the shed is studded with sharply pointed vertical laths or ridges. There the poor sufferer, barefooted and practically stripped of all clothing, was forced to endure a minimum period of 24 hours. Imagine his condition. He can see not the smallest space where he can either stand or sit; for everywhere his body comes into contact with the sharp protrusions. Thus the pitiful victim has to twist himself for 24 hours into a thousand postures, and when at last he issues forth from this infernal shed, he is exhausted, as though suffering from some grievous illness, and his whole body is covered with spots and blue streaks and furrows.

From all these things, gentlemen, you will understand how low and miserable I felt. I speedily lost any sense of joy over my release from the death sentence, and I cursed my Creator because He had not then permitted me to die. Oh! how rebellious man hates his own soul! If it were now so unbearable in the Julich stronghold, what would have been my condition, if God had thrust me, in accordance with my wish, into the everlasting prison! Here in Julich death could at least put an end to my misery; but where is the end of the suffering which they experience, who are sentenced by the eternal Judge? Truly, thence I would have longed to return to the punishment block at Julich, as to a paradise. But I gave this not the slightest consideration while I was cursing God and wishing myself dead. And yet—what an enigma is man—I dared not to take my own life. In spite of all my hatred of life, there lay something in the bottom of my heart which caused me to shrink back from suicide. That something was not the thought that I should after twenty years in any case be free once more, but it was the dim, I might even say almost mechanical recollection of what I had heard about death and eternity from my childhood days. The seeds of truth which praying parents scatter in the hearts of their children, put forth deeper roots than is commonly believed. Such, gentlemen, was at that time my experience. I had torn away from God completely, and yet a secret band held me to Him, a band of which I was unaware; a band which indeed I had myself not tied, but which God had permitted to be tied in my tenderest youth, through my gracious parents.

4

Self-destruction I would not entertain; but escape, yes, that was my first and my ever-present thought. With that intention I arose, and with the same I went to my bed. But courage was necessary to attempt such a thing! Should the undertaking fail, then not death, but the doubling of length of sentence was inescapable. I realised the risk of the enterprise and for a long time I wavered between daring and desisting. At last however I made my decision. It was on the 14th April 1836, the evening before Easter, that I resolved to put my purpose into execution. We were working that afternoon outside the citadel, occupied in digging a ditch. It was 3 o'clock. I chose a moment when the patrols were less observant, and asked one of them who stood close by me, if I could fetch a crowbar which lay at the far end of the excavation. Suspecting no danger he granted my request. I sprang into the ditch, and shielded thus by the embankment I fled like the wind. After half an hour, apparently without my flight having been noticed, I came to the Ellbach, a stream lying to the east of Julich. Without hesitation, for I knew the stream, I sprang into it and concealed myself beneath its hollow bank in the shrubbery. I had lain there scarcely ten minutes when I heard footsteps and then voices.

"Where can the fellow be?"

"He must have hidden here among the bushes by the stream."

"Well then, you go along on that side, and I will go along this."

"You don't mean it? What does it matter about the fellow?"

"You're right; it's not much fun walking the length of this stream in the mud!"

"We had far better go into the next village and drink his health."

With these words the speakers departed, but there hung a drop of perspiration on every hair of my head. I remained as still as a stone until complete darkness had descended. Then I stood up, stiff with the cold, for I had literally lain down in a morass. After walking for ten minutes westwards, I came to the banks of the Roer. There I rinsed myself somewhat, and then hurried on. I was walking on quite blindly; for I was completely unacquainted with the roads. When I had walked for about an hour I found myself on the outskirts of a town which as I later learned is called Flossdorf. Two farmers approach me. Shall I speak to them? For your own peace of mind, thought I, do so, for otherwise you may but walk deeper and deeper into Prussia, and, after all, the object is to cross the border.

"Tell me, good friends, which is my quickest way to the Belgian frontier?"

The farmers stop and study me, insofar as the darkness permits, from head to foot. My clothing betrayed me at once.

"You have surely escaped from the citadel?" said they.

"Yes, O yes, but do not betray me," cried I.

"No, No! Have no fear, we have nothing against you. We give you our word that we will bring you over the border."

The tone in which these words were spoken was so kindly that my confidence was won immediately. I followed them, and they brought me to their home. There they provided me with somewhere to sleep and promised that they would take me further on my way at 2 o'clock in the morning. I shut not an eye, and when the clock struck two I was ready. The farmer's youngest son accompanied me to the border. At the break of day we came to the road from Maastricht to Aachen, whence we could see the Belgian village of Brokkerhausen.

"Here," said my guide, "I shall leave you. You see that little river yonder? That is the Wurm, which forms the boundary between Prussia and Belgium. You can now get with ease into Brokkerhausen which lies on the other side. God be with you!"

With these words he pressed into my hand 5 grosschen (a few pence), and hung over my shoulder a bag containing some bread and ham. I wanted to shake him by the hand, but he departed hurriedly. My eyes moistened as I watched him go. There was even then something within me which said: You do not deserve such loving treatment.

With my bundle on my shoulder and the five grosschen in my pocket, I walked in high spirits to the Belgian village. I met not a soul on the way, and neither was there yet a living mortal to be descried therein, apart from the cockerel which stood upon the dung-hill announcing joyfully the dawn of day. I recalled that it was Easter morning and realised that it would not be long before the verger would make his appearance in order to ring in the festive day. I made my way therefore to the church and sat down upon one of the tombstones in the churchyard. There I fell into a sweet reverie. You think, perhaps, gentlemen, that I realised the significance of sitting upon a tombstone on Easter morning! O no, no such thoughts entered my soul. I knew nothing of the true Resurrection. I only knew the resurrection from the grave of Julich. I felt free and breathed deeply. I bathed with satisfaction in the beams of the rising sun, which had never seemed to shine upon me in so friendly a manner as now. "Freedom!", I cried, "Freedom! What a royal treasure! The king of Prussia upon his throne is not richer or more happy than I am upon this tombstone." "But where do I go now?" thought I, when the initial excitement was over. "What am I going to do? I have no money, I have no substance, no friends and no well-wishers. Must I beg? O, but that is even worse than death. But there is nothing else to do."—My outlook became depressed over these considerations, and I felt that such freedom had after all, at bottom, little to recommend it. "You are free," said I to myself, "You are free—to beg, free—to die." These thoughts brought tears to my eyes. My heart was softened. I thought of my late dear mother and of some of the good things she had told me about. "Yes," said I with a sigh, "if you were still alive, I would still be able to sing, even here amid the tombs." I wept over my mother who was dead; but I spared not a thought for Him who liveth for ever. And all this upon Easter morning in the midst of tombstones!

I was stirred from my reverie by the arrival of the verger, who unlocked the church in order to ring the bell. I stood up and after a friendly greeting, took one of the ropes and helped him in this morning duty. Meanwhile I told him who I was and besought him to advise me how to act. The good man took me to his home, provided me with a cup of coffee, and said that I could not do better than to apply to the burgomaster for an identification paper, since I would otherwise be in danger of recapture.

By seven o'clock I was standing before the burgomaster.

"And what do you intend to do now?" said he, when he had listened to my story.

"Anything which the good Lord shall give me to do," I replied, "if I can but earn enough to keep the wolf from the door."

"That will not be easy for you in this part of the country," he continued. "We are flooded with Prussian deserters, and they are not very popular in this district. I can give you no better advice than to march to Brussels and take service in the Foreign Legion. You will then be serving France and can join the fighting in Spain. If you would like to do that, then I will give you an identification certificate with which you can get to Brussels. Once there you can present yourself before the Foreign Minister."

Though I knew very little about the Foreign Legion and the war in Spain, yet I understood enough to realise that I had little alternative to accepting the burgomaster's counsel. Furthermore there was something about the man which gave me confidence. His daughter also looked upon me with compassion, and as I left the house with the certificate in my hand, she gave me two francs, which were of great assistance to me on my journey. I shall not trouble you, gentlemen, with my difficult march via Tongeren to Brussels, since it contained nothing of unusual interest. In Brussels I was introduced to the minister of Foreign Affairs.

"Where do you want to go?" the minister enquired of me.

"Your Excellency," I answered, "be pleased to consider me entirely at your disposal."

"You are a deserter from Prussia. Therefore I will deal with you in accordance with normal instructions for deserters. Consequently you are to serve in the French Foreign Legion, and that for an indefinite period, according to the duration of hostilities."

To be brief then, I was given a billeting order, and the next day commenced to march via Lille to Nancy. There in its depot the French Foreign Legion was garrisoned, and I rejoiced not a little to come across many of my fellow-countrymen and companions in adversity, who like me were refugees."

5

Before we proceed with our deserter on his journey, we will leave him for a time resting at Nancy and make our readers a little more closely acquainted with the French Foreign Legion.

In the times of which we speak, unhappy Spain was ravaged by a persistent civil war. According to an old law of the land it had been determined that the sovereignty could not be in the hands of a woman; wherefore, should the king die leaving only daughters surviving, the government was to pass to his brother or his nearest kinsman. This law, known as the Salic law, should now have been brought into operation, when in 1833 King Ferdinand VII died, leaving only two daughters surviving. But Ferdinand VII had a wife named Maria Christina, who preferred making laws to keeping them. She had the king completely in her power, and it caused her little effort to move him, in spite of the Salic law, to declare in his will his eldest daughter Isabella as heir to his crown. It is true to say that Princess Isabella was yet but a child, but Maria Christina had also ensured that she herself, by the same testament, was declared Regent during her daughter's minority. Now if King Ferdinand had had no male kinsmen of any importance, then this whole plan may well have gone through without any trouble. But the king had a brother, Don Carlos, who was in no sense a man to be put upon. Don Carlos knew only that he was by right and by law the heir to the Spanish throne; and that he was correct in this opinion, was as clear as the sun in the heavens. Don Carlos however knew the ambitious character of his sister-in-law Maria Christina only too well; and though during the king's life the contents of the testament had been kept as secret as possible, yet Don Carlos had got scent of it, and had attempted to confer with his brother privately before he died. Maria Christina had forestalled this however by ensuring that the two brothers never met without witnesses. Thus then the last will and testament remained unaltered, with the result that upon Ferdinand's death the people had to choose between the Salic law and the Will of the late king.

One would think that there was not a man in the whole of Spain, who would for one moment hesitate in which of these alternatives to choose; for it went surely without saying that Don Carlos was the rightful heir to the throne. But it was in those times in Spain, so far as a conception of right and wrong was concerned, extremely outlandish. The Spaniards were far behind the other European nations in development and culture, and they lacked above all the blessed light of the Reformation, since the whole length and breadth of the land knelt under the papal sceptre. But although the good influence of the Reformation had not penetrated into Spain, the malignant French revolutionary spirit had indeed found an entrance, and this had brought about among the people something good and something evil: something good, in that it opened the eyes of many to the foolish and disgraceful nature of the priests' dominion; something evil, in that those same eyes became averse to the sovereignty of kings. In consequence of this there arose in Spain a strong liberal party which, in accord with French ideals, wished to put as much power as possible in the hands of the people. Opposed to this was another party, which ruled especially in the northern provinces of the state and which held tooth and nail for the old statutes and rights.

The liberal party was very numerous in the southern provinces, and particularly so in the state capital, Madrid. Even the highest assembly in the land, called the Cortes, which corresponds with our Parliament, consisted for the most part of liberal members. These of course were at the beck and call of Maria Christina since she sympathised with the French liberal spirit. When therefore the last will of the late king was opened, the Cortes was summoned to assemble, and they did not hesitate to declare young Isabella as queen and her mother Maria Christina as regent. Not a word was said about the Salic law, and that too was quite in accordance with the spirit of French liberalism; for it acknowledges as legal only that of which it approves.

Meanwhile Don Carlos did not let the grass grow under his feet. He protested publicly against the breaking of the Spanish laws; but he discovered that it is of little avail to protest against plunder, when the robbers themselves are the judges. He realised that he would have to maintain his rights sword in hand. He made his way therefore to the northern provinces where he had many supporters. This support resulted not only from attachment to his person, but also, and indeed chiefly, from sympathy for the cause he defended. Don Carlos was considered as the champion of the priestly power and of the old laws of the land, and in consequence the priest-serving inhabitants of the northern provinces were completely in his hand. Furthermore these districts had from old time been in possession of certain rights and privileges (known in Spanish as *fueros*), which Spanish kings, on ascending the throne, had always sworn to be inviolable. The inhabitants of these districts realised very well however that their privileges would cease if the French liberal spirit gained the upper hand in the land, and for this reason too they were so much the more on the side of Don Carlos, who had after all drawn his sword on behalf of the old Spanish laws. Within a short time Don Carlos had a standing army on the move, and he made such good use of it against Maria Christina and her supporters, that on two occasions he almost got to the point of taking Madrid by force of arms.

It was not however in the counsel and purpose of God that Don Carlos should mount the throne which was his according to the ancient laws of the land. The spirit of revolution which from France, fired the European peoples, was not favourable to his cause. Russia alone was the single power to acknowledge his rights; but Russia was too far distant to support him by deeds. The neighbouring powers on the contrary, namely France and England, did not refuse even to resist him openly and to take the part of Maria Christina. This was manifest not only from the fact that, in England as well as in France, serving soldiers obtained leave in order to go on Spanish service in Maria Christina's cause, but there were even auxiliary corps formed in both these lands which bore the name of Foreign Legions, and in which anyone who was not a Spaniard could take service.

This was corn in Egypt for countless deserters, vagrants, fortune-seekers, adventurers and all sorts of low types, who in this manner obtained an opportunity of earning a living by force of arms, of seeing foreign lands and of seeking plunder and booty; for it was patently obvious that in that unhappy land of Spain, burdened with civil war, there would be a great deal to see, to enjoy and to steal. Of the two Foreign Legions however, the English did not deserve the name, since it consisted mainly of English soldiers. There is not much to be said in their favour though, because the British government used this Foreign Legion as a channel to rid themselves of the filth and dregs of the land, placed within it all such as caused them perplexity. The French Foreign Legion, on the contrary, consisted for the most part of foreigners and was a general mixture of every single European nation.

All who in Germany, Poland, Belgium and Holland had run foul of the laws of the land and who needed to make good their escape, took flight to the French Foreign Legion, where, entered under some imaginary name, they could disappear without trace. It can readily be imagined what a disorderly and unruly troop that French Foreign Legion presented. In Spain it was a true band of robbers. The members of the compounded corps scarcely passed the Spanish border when they were virtually left entirely to their own devices. It is true they served for French pay, but this was very parsimonious and irregular, and they were usually forced to cater for their own means of subsistence. In this matter then they made no scruple of thieving and plundering all and sundry, and since frequently their officers were no better than the other ranks, this freebooter's life, provided it did not go to too great an excess, was winked at. In the war they were really violent men, who fought the Carlists (the supporters of Don Carlos) to the death. This was indeed necessary; for since they were foreigners, they could expect no pardon whatever, so they had but to choose between victory and death. It is easy to see what incalculable harm these Foreign Legions caused to the Carlists, and that they were instrumental in hastening the failure of Don Carlos' cause.

When at last, through various circumstances Don Carlos was forced to give up the fight and leave the country, the Foreign Legion was also dismissed. The greater part of the French Foreign Legion found itself towards the end of the war in a condition of abject misery. In a strange land, without friend or kinsman, hated by the whole population and at every moment laid open to the most traitorous and murderous attacks, these unhappy men had to spend night and day as outcasts continually in the open field and in the midst of the Pyrennean snows. Their joy can be appreciated, when at length the command came to leave this murderous land. Many even so found themselves in no small trouble, in that they knew not where to go; and it was for them a great relief that France just at that time once more thrust forth a new Foreign Legion to wage war in Algeria. In the course of our story we shall have an opportunity to return to this Algerian Foreign Legion; but now we must go back to our fugitive, whom we left in the depot at Nancy.

6

At Nancy, the speaker continued, I found many fellow-countrymen in a similar plight, and this gave me a cheerful outlook, particularly because they held out the most wonderful prospects in Spain. "Spain," said they, "is the most glorious country in the world. There they have every day hot chestnuts and venison. The wine, the wonderful Spanish wine, flows in streams down the mountains, and oranges hang from the trees by the side of the open road." There was some truth in the description, but not for miserable deserters such as we. That I discovered later from bitter, bitter experience. It became perfectly clear to me in Spain why the French, when they speak of building castles in the air, always say "You are building castles in Spain." Meanwhile however I believed everything, and as I had formerly passed God by, so yet again I had no longer the slightest need of Him. Spain had become my heaven, but a heaven—without God. God in His great mercy was about to teach me plainly that without God even a heavenly land becomes a hell.

When I had been in Nancy 13 days, the day arrived upon which the fortnightly draught of 35 men marched off to Spain. I was included among their number. The marches which we made lasted between five and seven hours and were generally quite bearable. Of course they were, for we were going to our heaven and were happy and in good heart, and felt no fatigue. After a series of forty two marches we arrived on the 26th July 1836 at Pau, a little town on the border between France and Spain, at the foot of the Pyrenees. Here we were taught how to use French arms and within three weeks we were trained. In August we filed over the Pyrenees to Pamplona, the capital of Navarra; soon afterwards we came under fire near Barbastro. There I had my first whiff of gunpowder, and when the bullets whistled so close by me, I began to realise that there were other things to be met besides oranges along the open road. My heart began to tremble a little and once again my gracious parents and their prayers came to my mind. I began to think of a heaven other than the Spanish one, but these impulses lasted little longer than twenty four hours. When I had got away from the smell of the powder and a refreshing draught had swilled the shock from my heart, I was the old sinner once more. In a second engagement, which took place near Ponte la Reine, I was already a hero, who cared for neither death nor the devil; but I must admit that my courage was chiefly due to the wine, which was scarcely away from my lips all day. The whole of the year 1836-37 passed by with all sorts of small skirmishes. We were generally used for mere robbery of the countryside, and appeared to be intended chiefly to cause damage to the Carlists where possible by plunder and killing.

I had dreamed of the Spanish heaven, and in truth, so far as the scenery was concerned, I had not been deceived. The province of Navarra especially, where we spent most of our time, was a grand and fruitful highland district. Everything which is planted there grows luxuriantly, demanding the minimum of attention from the peasants. The mountains are clad with ever fresh and green shrubs and stout fir or beech trees. The most beautiful flowers, untouched by human hand everywhere adorn the fruitful soil. Not only did I notice there many of our German shrubs, but the most lovely plants whose blooms would certainly have ornamented the gardens of our landed gentry. The brown tulip with her yellow streaks was particularly abundant, and other white flowers unfolded their velvety leaves to fill the air with the most pleasing scents. In a word, God had suffered nothing to lack which could make the land like a paradise, but here as in every place it was man who turned the paradise into a wilderness of thorns and thistles. It would be almost impossible to suffer poverty here if they would but take the trouble once a year to plant and to harvest, but even this is too much trouble for the idle folk who inhabit these parts. Green vegetables grow here almost wild. The peasants usually make them into soups which they spice strongly with salt and pepper.

Now, pepper is here commonplace; for Spanish peppers are eaten with bread. At first my mouth would quite burn, but later I became accustomed to it and ate it like gingerbread. Wine is drunk even by the poorest. It might be thought that we would refresh ourselves with this gift of God; but what divine gift is there which a sinner abuses not? We were drunk virtually the whole night long, not with strong drink, but with "candilte", which we carried about with us all day long in casks. Yes, we even prepared our dinner with this wine, and the rice, which we ate daily, floated in the sap of the grape.

Despite the idleness of the people, I saw in that land of abundance, nevertheless the clearest signs of prosperity. It certainly appears as though God would constrain the people to repent through a concentration of blessings; but it is also apparent, how little the most abundant gifts of nature bring about repentance, as long as the heart of man hearkens not to the Word and the Spirit of God.

The farmhouses and village dwellings do not differ much from our own. The luxury in wearing apparel on the other hand, is very great. The ordinary women would be ashamed to wear a bonnet made of anything other than silk. The men are extremely fond of fine shirts and waistcoats, and a beggar would not be taken amiss for wearing a waistcoat in which a well-to-do man would be pleased to appear among us. It is a particular delight among the town and country dwellers to make themselves buttons from pieces of silver money, known as piacettas. Even the poorest tramp wears these coins on his clothing, and would rather die of starvation than cut them off to buy bread. In fact, hunger never reaches such a pitch in these parts as to make such a thing necessary; for God here casts foods, so to speak, at men's feet. Instead of giving Him thanks, as Christ teaches us to do, they offer their praises to saints' images and to priests. It is appalling to see how superstitious and idolatrous the people here have become. Within, and sometimes without the door of each house is to be found a holy-water stoup, and those who enter or depart make the sign of the cross.

We all had to imitate this whether we were Roman, Protestant, Christian or Jew, and woe betide us had we refused; we would not have survived for 24 hours. The priests here are literally worshipped. People do their utmost to kiss the hem of the priests' garment, and when a priest enters a house, having removed his shoes in the porch, then the servants and the children vie with each other to be able to kiss the shoes. As he walks along a street there is little else he does than to wave with his hand and to murmur in Latin by way of pronouncing a blessing. We never passed a church, no matter at what time of day, without seeing a swarm of people kneeling prostrate in the street. From this you might expect that they are guided in all their thoughts and actions by religion. But no! it is almost a daily occurrence for someone to be murdered in a church. Murder and treachery are indeed the order of the day. Even the women carry daggers which are drawn and raised aloft on the slightest pretext. It was at that time quite common for a Christino to murder his brother in bed beside him for being a Carlist. There is thus very little or nothing of home or family life here. The women go out all day long to visit each other or to sit talking in groups somewhere on the roadside. The men do little other than to practise shooting and fencing and whoever can bear arms, takes sides either with Christina or Carlos, and sets out where possible to injure the opposing party.

7

You can well imagine, dear sirs, the situation in which we were placed, among such treacherous people! I call them treacherous because I have more than once seen with my own eyes a Spaniard make a friendly approach to one of our men as though he would have a heart-to-heart talk, only to thrust a dagger into his heart whilst in the midst of a conversation which contained no suspicion of a quarrel, and then to flee. I was myself frequently in danger of becoming the victim of such falsehood. I was once stationed for four months in Fetrille, a "Carlist" village. We were six men and one corporal, quartered in one house. This house was in our bad books, for there was a rumour that several soldiers had been murdered there. The household consisted of a mother and three daughters, who treated us with more hospitality than we had ever experienced in Spain. They could not do enough to tempt us with food, and were inexhaustible in their invitations as to what we would drink. I had not considered this to be merely from motives of hospitality however, and warned my comrades not to drink from any bottle which the women had not themselves first sampled, and to beware especially that we did not become intoxicated. Thus a few days and nights passed. At night of course we always took turns to keep watch by the door of our room. One Sunday I had gone to Chigno with two comrades. When we returned we noticed downstairs that several men were indoors, who were apparently trying to hide themselves from us. We acted as though we had not seen them; but on arriving upstairs in our room, we informed our colleagues of our suspicions.

"Do you not know how many there are?" asked the Corporal.

"No, I saw them but at a glance. There could as well be twenty as three."

"Twenty! Then we are lost."

"How shall we act?" was the anxious question.

"Fellows," said one, "we must set to with drawn swords. If we wait until nightfall we are certainly lost. At the moment we have a chance of risking life or death."

We felt that this was the best counsel, so with loaded rifles and drawn sabres we went below.

"Woman," said the Corporal to the mother, "you have men indoors. Where are they?"

The woman vowed before God and all the saints that there was no-one within, but herself and her daughters, and brought out at once a bottle of wine. We were not to be fooled, however and made a search of the house. For an hour we ferreted in every gap and corner, but found nothing. We were on the point of returning to our room when one of us had the thought to thrust aside a large linen cupboard, which we had already inspected, and which stood against a wall. He had scarcely done this when we noticed a door in the wall, which, when we had opened, revealed a built-in cupboard from which issued three men armed with daggers. We seized them at once, bound their hands behind their backs and would, without trial, have shot them through the head had not the three daughters cast themselves with great clamour between us and cried: "They are our three brothers! They are Christians and have concealed themselves because they have murdered two Carlists!" To be brief, we released the poor fellows under their vow that they would never return. Meanwhile we redoubled our watch and lay for a further three months with loaded guns and bared swords at night on our mattress, while one of us kept watch continually. We even secured the door of our room with chains and bars. At last we were posted and replaced by six other men of our corps. These made fun of our safety precautions and threw the chains and bars out of the window. But when the next morning dawned, three of them lay murdered in their beds.

From all these things, gentlemen, you will realise that relations between the Foreign Legions and the general populace were anything but good. We were feared like devils, and wherever we appeared, all fled before us like children before a bully. We acted indeed as such. When we entered a village, the mayor was pressed to provide victuals. If he refused, or if he did not act with due speed, then the plundering was from the first house to the last, and we had frequently begun to plunder while the quartermaster was yet on his way to make arrangements with the mayor. The inhabitants for their part were naturally intent on revenge. It was the young girls who were made use of for this purpose. Secreting a poignard beneath their clothing, they would make the soldiers merry, knew how to allure them to a lonely spot, and there murdered them in cold blood. Amid such circumstances, as you can well suppose, we led the most miserable existence. We hung continually between life and death. There was moreover the misery of poverty and the climate, which in winter in the upper Pyrenees is raw and extreme. After the engagement near Ponte la Reine our first real sufferings began, and the Spanish heaven became a hell. We had to bivouac the whole winter in the mountains; we spread our straw pallets in the snow, and during the day we had to search for food. I suffered fearfully from hunger and thirst, and walked about almost naked. By reason of our camp life, the French uniform had quickly worn out; I had nothing more than a torn greatcoat and a pair of trousers with twelve patches, teeming with vermin. We were left completely to our own devices, for our money had for some time remained unpaid. Thus then we were real robbers in a land which abhorred us like the pest. There was not a shadow of religion among us, for we had no chaplain. I often knew not which day of the week it was, for not a thought was given to Sundays or Festival days. In this distress we were forced daily to leave a number of our comrades behind in the snow, because their feet were frost-bitten and there could be no thought of transportation to a hospital.

These unhappy sufferers would then beseech us to put a bullet through their heads rather than leave them to a protracted agony. To such a deed however we could not bring ourselves and thus left them to a lingering death. How often I envied them however, for death was to me there better than life. At last the misfortune struck me also, which had already cost thousands their feet. We were however, close to Saragossa at the time, so that I could be transported.

There I entered the hospital, where I remained until February 1838. Happily my feet recovered, but I expected to starve; for in hospital we were given just as much food as was absolutely necessary to prevent death. You can imagine then what good tidings it was for me to learn that peace had been signed and that the Foreign Legion would be disbanded. With a rejoicing heart I journeyed to Pamplona, whence we were escorted to Pau. Here we were once more on French soil. We were released from service by the burgomaster, but without any travel allowance. I was now free; but—free only to beg. Where was I to go? I had obtained new clothes indeed, but that was all. The only thing left to do was to take the advice of the burgomaster. We learned from him that France was forming a new Foreign Legion for service in Africa. I had never been to Africa, but amongst my companions were many who had served there, and what they had related of their experiences made me anything but anxious to try it. I was still full of the sufferings in Spain and thought: No, I would rather beg than go to Africa. Thus I wandered about undecided for a few days and finally declared to the prefect that on no conditions would I take service. Hereupon he gave me a "Passport of incapacity" (passeport d'indigence) as far as Strasburg. There were five of us; besides myself, two Dutchmen and two other Germans. So it came about that we walked as beggars from one end of France to the other, and in April we arrived shoeless and with rent clothes, looking like real vagabonds in Strasburg.

8

Thus after indescribable sufferings in Spain, I was again on the borders of Germany; and how my heart hankered to step over the frontier and see my fatherland once more! My two German fellow-travellers could not resist this temptation; they left us and entered Germany. I dared not attempt it however; still less my two Dutch comrades; for they were deserters and if they returned, could look for fifteen years imprisonment. We entered a beggars' asylum, but the warden became angry when he noticed that we neither had a penny in our pockets, nor would we go out begging. "Listen friends," said he, "I cannot keep you for nothing. If you can lay hands on something, it matters not to me how you do it, as long as you bring it to me. But if I were in your state, you are still young fellows, I would join the African Foreign Legion. Then at least you would have money in hand and be free from misery." I saw indeed that I would have to bite through the sour apple. In despair I sat down at the table with my head in my hands.—"Come," grumbled the warden, giving me a push, "You must get out; for if you don't bring me at least a half franc today, I will put you out in the street with an empty stomach."

I sprang up convulsively and ran out of the door. Within an hour I was back with money in my hand. I had signed on for Africa. But it lay like lead on my heart and I cursed my precipitance. Looking back however it has become clear to me why I was to do this. God had sent me to Spain to break my heart there; but that stony heart returned thence as unbroken as when it had entered. I needed even heavier blows, and therefore God gave me over to my own foolish way. Yet how merciful and longsuffering is Divine Grace, in leading a sinner to repentance! I did everything I could to make conversion, humanly speaking, impossible; but everything which I considered evil was indeed used of God to bring me to that place where I should bend my knees in the dust before Him, with a broken heart. To be brief, I appeared again on 3rd May in Nancy, where the Foreign Legion depot was situated. There we rested before a march to Toulon, in the south of France, which we reached 23rd June. We spent a further thirteen days in the "Chapeau Rouge" barracks. We then went aboard ship in a group of 175 men, and after a voyage of five days and five nights duration we entered the harbour of Algiers.

9

We permit ourselves a further small digression ere we accompany our fugitive further in his journey. The reader may perhaps require to know what business the French had at that time in Africa . . .

The city of Algiers had for centuries been a thorn in the flesh of the Christian states of Europe. Way back in the fifteenth century the Moors, who profess the Mohammedan religion, had made a nest there. The strong aspect of the city on the side of a mountain which slopes towards the sea made it an ideal headquarters for piracy. It was indeed with this end in view that the Moors had made themselves masters of it.

This was a veritable plague for European trade; for everything which sailed from Europe to the Levant must needs traverse the waterway where the pirate ships of these Algerian Moors cruised about. Unhappy was the vessel which fell into their hands. It was towed into Algiers, the lading was confiscated and the crew chained and enslaved. Whilst they then under the title of "Christian dogs", suffered the most cruel ill-treatment, torn from their wives and children and forced to spend their days in hard labour, the opportunity was given to buy their freedom. The sums which were demanded however, were so exorbitant, that the majority were forced to end their days in this fearful slavery. Algiers then was a wicked robber's nest and the grave of many a Christian seaman. At the head of this robber-state was a ruler who bore the title of the Dey. He ruled despotically, as was the ancient custom among the Mohammedans of the

East. His might increased with every century, and before long there was no power which was more feared than that horrible den of thieves, whose privateers respected no nation at all.

Our readers will be able to appreciate that the European powers soon considered some means to root out this weed; but this was easier said than done. In 1541 the powerful emperor Charles V made a crusade against Algiers; but he had so many hindrances that he returned with his mission unaccomplished. The French king, Louis XIV, attacked the city again in 1682 with a heavy bombardment; yet he succeeded no more than his predecessor. This prosperity made the Algerians even more proud and rapacious until at last they threatened to close the whole of Europe's sea trade.

Eventually this went to such a pitch that the English in union with the Dutch sent out a fleet in 1816, in order to teach the Dey a lesson. It was indeed a tremendous lesson which he received on this occasion; for his city was for the greater part shot to ruins and most of his fleet destroyed. His Mohammedan Highness now began to pluck different strings on his viol, and willingly agreed to release all Christian slaves, and henceforth to make no more prisoners of war into slaves, but rather to exchange prisoners in accordance with European usage. At the same time he had to promise to make the necessary contracts with the European powers, by means of which his relationships with them would rest on a more regular footing. From then on the privateering became generally less, though the smaller ships still sailed in continual danger, and many a vessel was secretly towed into the harbour of Algiers. Furthermore the Dey had stipulated for himself a certain toll or tax which he raised from passing shipping. For these and other reasons the powers in Europe resolved when the time should be ripe, to make an end of this Algerian state.

They merely waited for a suitable opportunity to present itself, and if we may believe the verbal traditions, as they have been passed down in Algiers, this opportunity presented itself very soon in the following manner.

Not far from old Carthage, also upon the African coast, but to the East of Algiers, lies another Mohammedan sea port, called Tunis, whose ruler bears the title of Bey. Now it came about that the Bey of Tunis wished to present to one of his favourite wives a beautiful piece of jewellery. In his city was a French Israelite, a jeweller by trade, to whom he gave the order for this expensive present. The jeweller had it manufactured in Paris and brought to the Bey of Tunis his bill for 30,000 francs. Whether the Bey had imagined that his foible would cost nothing like so much as this, or whether he had just at that moment suffered some terrible loss, is not clear; but at any rate he looked in vain among his treasures for the sum demanded and could think of no other solution than to give the jeweller a quantity of grain, free of tax, by way of payment. The Israelite was perfectly satisfied with this arrangement, for he saw every hope of disposing of this article at a profit. Indeed it was at that time that Napoleon was passing through Europe with his armies and he required for his soldiers large amounts of bread daily. Our Israelite came to an agreement with the army suppliers, who accepted his wares gratefully at a price in excess of 100,000 francs. Thus the jeweller had become in one moment a rich man. Only one thing was lacking, namely—the payment itself. And here it was that he experienced that there is nothing more fickle in this world than the much boasted fortune. Just at this moment Napoleon tumbled from his throne whence he found his way to the island of St. Helena. Louis XVIII replaced him on the throne, and to him the jeweller presented his bill. But whatever else Louis would or would not pay, with this bill he would have no truck.

Disappointed and convinced of the righteousness of his cause, the jeweller sought hither and thither for means to lay hands on his money. For this purpose he spent some years in making application to all powerful and influential personages from whom he could hope to get any assistance. Thus it was that he arrived one day before the Dey of Algiers whose protection and influence he sought for his cause. Possibly he had promised the Dey half shares if he should help him to obtain his money. At any rate His Mohammedan Highness did not hesitate to press the French Government repeatedly for payment of this bill. The French Government, however, merely answered these expostulations of the Dey with many compliments which said nothing. This grieved him, and he resolved to give another turn to the screw. A great Mohammedan feast was one day being celebrated in Algiers, at which it was the custom for the consuls of the foreign powers to be received in audience by the Dey. The French Consul, M. Duval, was among the honourable guests who filled the audience chamber. The Dey then turned towards him with the sudden question: "Tell me, sir, why it is that the Israelite jeweller cannot obtain recompense for his lawful debt from your government, though I have repeatedly pleaded his cause?"

Our readers must remember that the Dey expressed this question in the Arabic tongue: and the Arabic tongue is one not easily learned by a Frenchman. For this reason M. Duval normally made use of a translator when he had the honour to discuss matters of state with His Algerian Majesty. This occasion however was more in the nature of a festival gathering, hence M. Duval did not have his interpreter with him at the moment. He had however been long enough in Algiers to be able to understand what His rapacious Majesty was saying to him, and was able to put together enough Arabic to prevent the necessity of merely grinning at the Dey in incomprehension. He did his best then to gather from his stock of Arabic enough words to produce to the best of his knowledge an answer to the Dey which gave every hope of an agreeable settlement before very long. But our good French Consul in his ignorance used a few Arabic expressions which were quite unacceptable in the presence of a Prince and the gist of which were as follows: "What has this got to do with you, you Algerian sneak thief and cheat! Mind your own business and don't stick your black baboon face in other people's affairs." Whatever the case may have been, the Dey's face looked like thunder, and raising his long fan which he used normally to cool himself, he struck the French Consul in the face, giving him an eye as black as the skin of His Algerian Majesty himself. Now things began to move fast. The Dey of Algiers had offered insult to France, and the French Government took such a serious view of the matter that they declared war upon the Dey. The latter troubled himself very little about this at first, thinking doubtless to himself: "Here I am high and dry on the sea coast and I can easily keep these French leeches from my body." But this was a gross miscalculation of His rapacious Majesty. He experienced the truth of what another king had once said, who was wiser than he.

"There is no king saved by the multitude of an host; A mighty man is not delivered by his great strength. An horse is a vain thing for safety: neither shall he deliver any by his great strength. Behold the eye of the Lord is upon them that fear Him, upon them that hope in His mercy."

Psalm 33, vv. 16, 17, and 18.

The Dey of Algiers was not among those rare people who in trouble wait upon that unseen but mighty Ally. He relied on his own might, and, as always in such cases, he fell from his eminence into the sand. On the 5th July 1830 the French fleur-de-lys fluttered from the battlements of his palace. The Dey was sent into exile and ended his life in that ignoble condition.

All who traded by sea in Europe rejoiced on hearing the tidings that the Algerian robber's nest had been conquered and that an end had been made of the shameful privateering. Meanwhile in spite of the honour to French arms in this victory, the booty was not much to boast of, for the victors had nothing more than the city of Algiers in their possession. The Dey had indeed held sway over the surrounding lands known as the Regency, but the inhabitants of those places, Mohammedan at heart, were extremely unwilling to acknowledge the rule of the "French Christian dogs". These passionate people seized arms and resolved to dispute every inch of ground with the French. This would not have presented the might of France with much difficulty apart from two reasons which delayed their advance. The first was that just at the time of the conquest of Algiers, the French king Charles X was deposed by a revolt of his people, which resulted in a general upheaval of the land. It is true that Louis Phillipe who replaced him on the French throne, took good control of the situation, but his hands were thereby so well occupied that he had at first no time to think of Algiers. The second reason for the check in the progress of victory in Africa was the unhealthy, scorching heat followed by sudden cold which typified the Algerian climate, and to which the European soldiers were unaccustomed.

Furthermore, the Moorish tribes who lived in these countries, among whom the Kabyles were the most powerful and cruel, possessed a complete knowledge of the terrain, and practised on this terrain a method of warfare to which the French soldiers could never get accustomed. These Moorish tribes, being of Arabic origin, led a wandering shepherd's life just as of old did the patriarchs, Abraham, Isaac and Jacob. In at least one particular they differed from the patriarchs, namely they bore not only the mild shepherds' crook, but the sword of battle also. Mounted upon their swift horses, they fly through the wilderness like an arrow from the bow. None can equal their horsemanship, for they are almost born and bred in the saddle. They take aim while riding at full speed, and seldom miss their mark. When they unite to give battle they charge upon their foe at a flying gallop, stop suddenly at a distance of twenty yards, fire their rifles, wheel their horses at lightning speed, and before the enemy can return fire they have gone like the wind. In this manner, by turns, attacking and fleeing they charge their foes, like grasshoppers, from all sides and it is easy to judge how murderous and exhausting such warfare must have been for the French soldiery. The combination of circumstances thus made the condition of the French army very difficult at first, and in urgent need of improvement.

As soon as peace had been restored in France, Louis Phillipe hasted to attend to this necessity. He sent a mighty army to Africa which made a start under the command of marshal Clausel, of warring with the bellicose tribes. It is common knowledge that the French soldiers are a force to be reckoned with; nevertheless it was nearly twenty years before they had cleared the narrow stretch of land of all enemies. It was in particular the renowned, enthusiastic and intrepid Emir, Abd-El-Kader, who kept them occupied for years. This indefatigable foe gave them not a moment's respite, but attacked them incessantly at the head of numerous tribes which he aroused with religious fervour to rebel against the "Christian dogs". It will perhaps never be known what was the cost to France of being able to retain these Algerian colonies in her possession, because the records of Government expenses, for reasons of state, are not very reliable. From what is known however, it can be sufficiently proved that the loss of life must have been fearful. Added to this was the fact that the colony, instead of producing profit, was costing unmentionable sums each year, so that the French Cabinet was often on the point of giving up the whole colony. It was feared however that England would then make herself mistress of the territory; and rather than permit such a thing to happen, they were prepared to put up with the greatest sacrifices.

We must add to this that the fighting methods of the warring parties differed greatly. This was particularly noticeable in the barbaric manner in which the Africans handled their prisoners. At first no quarter was given; a premium was paid for each head; later, when ransom-money was paid for prisoners-of-war, life was spared, but prisoners were exposed to such terrible ill-treatment, that they perished notwithstanding.

It was scarcely surprising that the French soldiers began to handle their prisoners in a similar fashion. This was especially true of the light troops, called up for this campaign, the infantry being mainly the Foreign Legion, and the Cavalry consisting in part of native allies, and in part of French soldiers who required strong discipline. These troops, who added no small weight to the successful outcome of such expeditions, were gathered from a multitude of adventurers from all lands. It was necessary to form a separate Corps for these men. The normal military penal code and normal discipline were too soft for them, who had to be held in like beasts with bit and bridle, with extraordinary severity. The punishments which were invented for them were so terrible that the Minister of War was attacked about them in the Chamber of Deputies, and he was forced to have an enquiry made by a commission of members of the Chamber, the result of which being that, gruesome as the treatment was which these soldiers underwent, it had to be admitted that the Corps could not be controlled by any other means. On the field of battle however they were invaluable against the Kabyles, for they stopped at nothing.

We return from our digression and follow our narrator on his journey.

10

"When I arrived at Toulon, I sighed deeply. I felt that I was but a poor, miserable vagabond, and I could not think of my former peaceful life in my fatherland without feelings of great distress. Even so, my thoughts did not rise much higher than my earthly fatherland, and the mournful impressions lasted but a short while. The new land, the new continent which I should shortly be seeing, caused me great excitement. We were very soon on the steam ship which was to take us over the Mediterranean to Algiers. For me this was a new life. I had never seen the sea before, and I was therefore at first quite thrilled with these strange adventures.

Even so, I must admit that I felt by no means at home in the rough way of life which ruled on board. I had become used to many irregularities; in Spain I had seen things, gentlemen, which would certainly fill you with horror, but such barbarity and ill-manners as prevailed here on board, I had never before experienced. I could scarce believe my eyes, when I saw among the crew half-naked bedouins and negroes; at first I thought they were wild animals, and the manner in which they behaved was often so beastly that I blushed at the sight. I was therefore heartily pleased when at last, after a journey of five days and five nights, we cast anchor at 8 o'clock one morning in the harbour of Algiers. The impression made upon me by the city of Algiers, as viewed from the harbour, was indescribable; I thought I saw before me a city of magic palaces. Imagine a large number of white buildings lying between orange and fig trees against the sides of a mountain, so that the whole can be viewed from the harbour, just like the amphitheatre of an arena, stretching to the summit of the mount in a steeply sloping ascent. Above glitters the castle of the Dey, called the Casba Cabace, which at that time was used as a citadel. Behind the city rise the high peaks of the blue Atlas Mountains, which form the backdrop to this charming scene. I was completely transported. But what is more shortlived than the transport of a miserable deserter, who lacks the fear of God?

I was garrisoned until further orders in the Casba. On the third day there was a roll call, and 500 men were selected to serve between the city and the Atlas Mountains, a distance of 12 hours' march from Algiers. There was in fact a sort of fortress built on the Atlas Mountains, close to Sondougne. All the materials, lime, sand, timber and stone had to be taken thither from the city; for the fortress there being erected was in the middle of a desert. It was an extremely difficult task to transport anything in this wilderness; for the Kabyles lost no opportunity of hindering it. For this reason each transport was accompanied by 500 men. At the roll-call the old Spanish soldiers were selected first, and I was therefore brought into active service at once. I was so weak however that I was hardly able to go, for on the second day I had contracted shingles, the usual complaint of new arrivals, from which half of them usually died. How often I later wished that I had been numbered under them! Yet it pleased my God to spare my life, and now I can daily give Him thanks for that. Within eight days I had recovered, and I therefore had to join these fatiguing marches. Yes, fatiguing marches indeed! Never have I served in harder duties. In Europe we consider it unbearably hot when the thermometer shows 30°C. in the shade; but here the temperature stood between 38° and 42°. We departed early in the morning, heavily laden from Algiers, in this insupportable heat.

Towards midday we came to the Piemontrel plain, the limit of the French territory. Thence we had to proceed through the Arabic domain to the Atlas Mountains. That was like a journey through the valley of the shadow of death. While our time was occupied in loading and firing, in order to keep the Arabic horsemen at bay, we had also to push forward, though wet with perspiration and languishing for thirst amidst a thousand deaths and dangers. From time to time one or other of our men would fall in the sand, either overcome by exhaustion and fatigue or struck by a murderous Arabic bullet; and those who fell were left there to lie; they were not given another thought. We had not a moment's rest the whole day; whoever wanted to eat or drink had to fend for himself. Thus it was that towards eight o'clock one evening we arrived at our destination. Here we had two or three hours' rest to warm some soup.

Those who still possessed a little strength made a fire and set on a kettle. Often there was nobody who did even this; for it was not seldom the case that we fell to the ground with our packs on our backs and went to sleep. Towards midnight we again awakened and then would commence the return journey to Algiers, which was reached by 2 o'clock in the afternoon of the next day. There we could rest until the following morning, only to commence the same journey once again. For seven months I endured this, but, gentlemen, God Himself knows how fearful are the sufferings of such an existence. Continually under fire, across thickets and rocks, along tracked or untracked paths, with bleeding feet, lungs scarcely breathing, the tongue often hanging from the mouth, at night exposed to the cold shivering dew, in the daytime to scorching heat, provided with one bottle of water and wine—thus travels the soldier of the French Foreign Legion in Africa. If he gets into barracks in Algiers, then he must literally scrape away handfuls of vermin from his straw pallet, ere he can stretch out his tired limbs thereon. There is also in these parts a stinging insect which often bereft me of sleep in spite of exhaustion. How frequently I have prayed God that I might be hit by the first bullet. How often I have myself placed the muzzle to my own mouth—only to find that I had not the courage to take my life. Even then there was a terror of God in my heart. Such sufferings even as these in Algiers were not sufficient to destroy completely the seeds which my dear parents had scattered in my heart in the days of my youth.

It was commonly reckoned that of every fifty soldiers who had to take part in these harassing expeditions, forty five succumbed within six months. The strong constitution which God had given me, withstood for a long period the wasting effects both of the climate and the fatigue; but at last my powers also refused to perform their function. I fell ill, as it happened, just when we had returned to Algiers from an expedition. I found therefore a place in the lazaret,* or hospital, which had been set up in the Dey's garden. There, in a state of utter exhaustion, and lying at the gates of death, I was brought for the first time to a solemn consideration.

I spent many a sleepless night in considering those things for which, as I thought, I had hitherto never had the time. I reviewed my whole life, and began to realise that I was myself the cause of my miserable condition. "It is your own fault," said I to myself, "Your parents pointed out to you as a child the ways of God, but you have forsaken God. When you became a soldier, you gave yourself up to drink and pleasure, and God is therefore giving you up now to misery and death. Seek God, and He will have mercy upon you." Thus I thought in some of the better moments; but at other times I would again begin to murmur. "It really

* Lazaret, or lazaretto, originally a hospital for lazars or beggars with leprosy, hence, a hospital for the poor.

does seem unfortunate," said I then, "that I have to endure such a hard way of life. What numbers there are, no better than myself, who enjoy life to the full in peace and plenty; and I have surely done nothing so terribly wicked. I have not murdered or robbed; and many a thief, who has earned a bullet ten times over, is dressed in silks and satins, while I lie here, a wretched creature on a hard straw pallet, dragging out my miserable life in sighs and tears."

Such was the manner in which the evil one choked the good seed which sometimes began to germinate in my heart. I was totally unwilling to consider that I was a sinner before God, and that all my righteousnesses were unto Him but as filthy rags. I compared myself with those who I considered worse than I was, and not with the Lord Jesus, who knew no sin, and yet who, notwithstanding, had suffered immeasurably greater smart than anything I had experienced. I stood alongside the Pharisee in the temple and thanked God that I was not as other men; and I did not realise that God's hand was pressing down upon me, with the loving purpose of bending me into the attitude of the publican who cried "God, be merciful to me a sinner!" In this state of blindness I often disputed with my Maker and blamed Him for not putting a stop to my sufferings by death.

11

When I had lain for twenty-eight days in the lazaret, I was fully recovered and returned to the Casba. Though I had disputed with God, yet He was pleased not to repay me according to my sins, but even to bring some relief in my sufferings. Now I was promoted, and thus released from the murderous transports to the Atlas Mountains. I was now posted to Bougie, a citadel on the west coast of Algiers, and which we reached after a voyage lasting two days and three nights. When I had remained there in quarters for four months, from February until May 1839, I was sent with a number of men on an expedition to Chilchili. The heat of battle was intense, and now for the first time I really saw how devilish the Arabs are in war.

The Duke of Orleans, who later came to a sudden end in Paris, had at that time just arrived in Africa to fight in the war. He was by Chilchili with his army, and was shut in and blockaded by the Arabs. The purpose of our expedition then, was to relieve him; but you may well believe, sirs, that this was no simple matter. The Arabs fought for their lives and gave no mercy. Seated on their swift horses, they fire their long pieces with amazing dexterity, and every shot hits its mark. Scarcely is the report of the weapon heard however, than the horse wheels unbidden and disappears with its rider like an arrow from a bow. I assure you that not a few of our men perished in this affray. For the first time in my life I too was wounded; I had a shot in my left thigh. The injured were taken away on stretchers upon mules, and the seriously wounded in carts. Since I could still move, however, I bound my wound, which was through and through, with my kerchief, and hobbled on my right leg away from the fighting. There I met a donkey driver, or in other words, a supply-soldier, who was going to the camp with an unladen donkey. There hung a seat of sorts on each side of the donkey, and while a wounded Italian took his place in one, I placed myself upon the other. I could not endure it for long however, since every step the beast took caused the blood to gush from my wound; I was suffering unbearable pain. So I dismounted again and hobbled back to Chilchili. My clothes were soaked in blood.

I fell down in the road from weakness, and there I remained for some time, senseless. I neither heard nor saw any more; and it was only due to God's wonderful keeping, that I was not broken under the horses' hooves or under the wheels of the carts and cannons. But God showed unto me how He fulfils His own commandment! "Love your enemies, bless them that curse you, do good to them that hate you." He watched over me with a tender care, which I have only since realised with gratitude. When I had lain for some time unconscious, I was discovered by two comrades, who bound up my wound and carried me to the camp. They could do no more; they placed me on a bed and hurried back to the battle. There I awoke and was overcome by raging thirst. There was nobody near me, however, and thus I lay for two hours in terrible pain and unbearable thirst. At last an orderly appeared, who gave me a glass of lemonade, the drink which was here given habitually to the sick. I can still remember the wonderful refreshment which these draughts provided. I can in some small measure understand how our Saviour must have suffered when He cried, after so much loss of blood, "I thirst!" Yet He was granted nothing but vinegar to quench His thirst.

The next day I was taken by ship to the hospital at Bougie. If I was maddened with thirst at Chilchili, here I was almost starved. The French doctors prescribe to their patients a diet which is almost more dangerous, and certainly less bearable than their ailment; or rather the orderlies interpret these dietary prescriptions in such a severely extended manner as almost to make the services of the doctors superfluous. For thirteen days I had nothing other than lemonade; that was my food and drink. When I spoke of hunger, I was laughed to scorn, yes, was even threatened with punishment, if I did not keep quiet. Under these circumstances it was impossible for my wound to heal, and I began to think that the treatment was intended to do away with me by starvation. I was indeed prepared for death when the major began at last to realise that the first condition of healing was that the patient should remain alive, and he then ordained that I should receive a quarter ration of food per day.

Now at last my thigh began to heal. As soon as I had reached the stage of being able to rise, my first struggles were directed to stealing food whenever I saw the chance of procuring it. In my tormenting hunger I dragged myself along the beds and eagerly gathered every little crumb I could from the ground. This did me much harm however. The exertion caused my wound to re-open and to become inflamed. I had to lay flat on the bed again, and had nothing but lemonade for another seven days. I then discovered that my own company held guard at the hospital. For such a starving creature as I then was, this was joyful tidings. My wound had once more closed, and one night I crept outside and found an acquaintance on guard duty, marching to and fro before the gate. I made known to him my dire state of need, and he helped me to a few slices of dry bread. O, what riches were these! I began to weep for joy. I threw myself on my pallet, placed part of the bread thereunder, and ate the rest in such a state of happiness, as though I had won the whole world. Yes, dear sirs, when a man is really hungry he does not long hesitate to appropriate bread. Yes, though he is offered none at all, yet he drags himself outside at night, even with a sick body, to look for it. How many there are to whom better bread is held forth than that which perisheth, but who receive it not! Believe me, they may say that they hunger, but they are lying—that was my experience when I started to hunger indeed.

When I had remained for three months in the hospital, I was again restored to active service and was joined to the armed force which set out to overcome the citadel of Constantine. The tremendous siege, upon which at the time the eyes of the whole world were directed, it was my lot to experience. Here too God spared me in the most striking manner. For three whole days our heaviest pieces thundered against the city, until at last a breach was formed. When the breach was made, the General stepped forward and asked if there were ten men with the courage to enter and find out whether it was passable. We did not know whether the Arabs had formed from within a mine under the breach in order to blow us up as soon as we entered. Not one man volunteered however, and the General then commanded that two battalions of African troops and two battalions of Zouaves (Algerian Volunteers), were to penetrate the breach, while our battalion was to cover the rear. The two African battalions and the following battalion of Zouaves stand in the breach, when—boom!—everything before our eyes is blown sky-high. Of the three battalions not a man remained alive, and the shock threw us into some confusion. The Arabs had blown the mine, but one minute too soon; one minute later and we would all have met our death in the same terrible circumstance. In our battalion we numbered a hundred wounded, but I had come off without a scratch.

We now forced our way with fixed bayonets through the breach. There was a storm of bullets. At eight o'clock in the morning of the 20th September 1839 we carried the breach, but now the real battle was to begin. Every house in the city had been converted into a citadel and from every door and window cannons and guns belched forth death and destruction. Women stood with pans of boiling water or seething oil, with burning pitch and all kinds of deadly implements upon the roofs working diligently to accomplish our destruction. At the same time the streets were impassable, for in all directions there were piles of stones, carriages, wagons, felled trees and so forth, behind which the Arabs had crept, in order to continue their murderous fire. Every step in advance had to be bought with blood, and it was mid-day before we could plant the French flag in Fatima Square. Then at last we were conquerors. The Arabs left the city by the Fatima Gate, and ever since has Constantine been a French possession.

God having preserved me from all these mortal dangers, we were sent back to Bougie. The following year, it was 5th May 1840, I was again wounded in a battle on the plain of Mehaza. We had a fierce engagement there with the Kabyles, those naked demons of the wilderness, who wear nothing but an apron of animal skins; truly a savage people who seem to have been born for battle and who fear no peril. It was to my advantage that I was hit early in the battle; for now I had to be carried away from a fight in which nearly all my comrades met their death. I had been wounded again in the same thigh as formerly; but in a slightly lower position. Once again I was starved in the lazaret for seven months. When at last I was restored, my period of service was very nearly completed, and on the 29th May 1841 I departed for Algiers to sign off. I received fifty eight francs from the savings bank and obtained a map of the route to Toulon and Lille.

After a journey of some difficulty I arrived back in Belgium. My heart longed for my fatherland, and I would indeed have fled across the border willingly. The fear of being betrayed held me back however.

I resolved therefore to remain in Belgium and never to return to Prussia. But what is the resolve of man? "A man's heart deviseth his way: but the Lord directeth his steps." When God has determined to bring us to a certain place, of what avail are our resolves to the contrary! And how wonderfully God can use our own foolishness and sinfulness as a means of bringing us to the very place which He designs!

12

In the village of Dalheim, close to Verviers, I was able to find work as a farm labourer, and could thus at least buy some necessary clothing; for I looked like the king of all the beggars. I had worked here for six months when I became acquainted with a Walloon girl. I was extremely fond of her, and even thought in terms of marriage; but there was one difficulty; she had formerly been engaged to the son of the burgomaster, and he was still quite unable to keep his eyes away from her. It was the evening of New Year's day, while I was in the Walloon home, when the burgomaster's son entered. You will realise, gentlemen, that our meeting was by no means friendly! Five minutes had scarcely passed, when we commenced a battle of words, during which he called me a Prussian deserter. "You ought to be ashamed of yourself," said he to the Walloon girl, "for having any relationship with such a character, who has run away from a Prussian punishment cell." These words were hardly out of his mouth when my fists put him to a painful silence, and I gave him such a cuff round each ear that he fell to the floor. Boiling with rage, he demanded at once that honour be satisfied with pistols, and since my blood was up too, I accepted the challenge with equal readiness.

Next morning at eight o'clock I made my way to the house of his father, the burgomaster, who was already fully acquainted of the matter. The old man received me as though I had come to fetch his son for a country ramble.

"Sit down," said he, "my son will be here any minute; are your witnesses here?"

"Yes," said I, with some emotion, for though I had not the most sensitive of natures, yet it struck me forcibly, that a father could speak with such familiarity about his son's foolishness, yes, and could even give it his approval Meanwhile the son arrived, and before long we were each armed with a pistol. We now set out for the place agreed for our duel. On the way my heart sank within me. I was quite unskilled in the use of a pistol, and felt quite certain that my opponent was far better acquainted with the weapon than myself. "Great God," I thought, "am I now to end my life in such a manner, over a miserable argument about the hand of a fair woman." You see gentlemen, I knew not as yet the right consideration of death and eternity. Even so, I thought not so lightly as my opponent did of the matter; for he walked at my side as though he was on the way to a rabbit shoot.

"Friend," said I to him, "would it not be better if we turned back? What advantage is it to us to shoot each other through the heart, or to shatter arm or a leg?"

"No, no," he replied gruffly, "you cannot get away with it as easily as that. It is a point of honour. You have stained my honour, and that stain can only be removed by blood."

I made some further attempts to bring him to a change of mind, but in vain. At length we arrived at the appointed place, removed our outer clothing and placed ourselves twelve paces apart. Thus we stood like true Cains, ready to send each other into eternity. I made one more attempt.

"Consider," said I, raising the pistol, "that I have the first shot. If you will but give me the hand of reconciliation, I will shoot into the air."

"It is not a matter of consideration," he cried, "It is a matter of honour, and that to me is more than life itself."

"Well," said I, "Then I will forego my right. You shoot first. I have no desire to be your murderer."

This he accepted, took aim, fired, and shot me in my left upper-arm. Now I was furious and my merciful intentions gave place to boundless vengeance. In my turn I directed the barrel of my weapon towards him, and shot him under the heart in the lower part of the body, so that the bullet came out at the back. While he was borne away dead, I made for my lodgings. It was not long before the officers of the law came to fetch me, and the next day my case was heard. I was held for five weeks under arrest and I expected nothing less than the sentence of death. I did not however know the Belgian laws relating to duels, and did not realise that the evidence produced by the witnesses was entirely in my favour. The decision of the judges was that I had been forced into the duel quite against my will, and had made every endeavour to prevent bloodshed; as a result of which they declared me "not guilty". Upon this I was set free and considered myself fortunate to get away with a fright. But ah, gentlemen, though I had been released from the sentence of human laws, I was and remained a murderer in the eyes of God's law. I was little concerned about this however; but later, when God opened my eyes, this sin caused a heavy burden of guilt, for which I have pleaded divine pardon upon my knees.

While thus once more escaping a great danger, little thinking what great mercy God was shewing such a man-slayer, I thought only of how I could go on living in as happy a manner as possible. It came into my mind that I was now not far from Aachen where six years before I had been garrisoned. I still had many friends and acquaintances there, and the desire arose to pay them a visit. I imagined how amazed they would be to see me again—one whom they must long ago have given up for dead. At the same time there was one great difficulty. Should I be recognised, all was lost. "But," thought I, "whoever would betray you? And what gain would it be to the Prussian Government to imprison you? They are sure to act as though they do not know you, and then you can spend a few carefree days with your friends." To be brief, I resolved to take the risk and the week before Easter in 1842 I made my way to Aachen.

13

Arriving there, I sought out my old acquaintances and prepared for a right joyful reunion. But I knew not by what cords an Almighty and faithful God was drawing me, a stubborn and rebellious sinner. My miseries in Spain and Africa had been so many hammer blows to break my heart of stone; but thus far they had been bestowed upon me without effect. Had the love of God been like that of men, then long ago He would have lost patience with me; but the love of God to a sinner whom He intends to save, knows neither diminishing nor faintness. This I was now again to experience, that I might become a monument of that stupendous mighty grace of God. Again the Divine hand stretched forth the rod to chastise me sore, and, gentlemen, looking back, I cannot thank a long-suffering God enough, that He did not esteem it too much to concern Himself with me again. Scarcely had my friends come to know that I, the deserter from the Julich citadel, had returned to the land, when the gendarmes arrived that same evening to arrest me. It was the 26th March, on Easter eve, when I was brought back to the fortress of Julich. The court martial lengthened my sentence by a year on account of my desertion, and thus once again I was shut up in the Julich citadel, there to undergo 21 years of penal servitude.

I was without hope or comfort. Tearing the hair from my head, I cast myself upon the floor of my cell, and considered how I might take my own life. But even then I had less heart for such a step as formerly. My unyielding and rebellious heart sought comfort rather in its own strength once more. "You are still young and strong," said I to myself, "and you have learned so much in Spain and Africa, that you can quite easily get away from these Prussian soldiers. You have escaped once, surely you can do it again; but then make sure that you get away to America." In such resolutions I found new comfort, and with such courage I set to work once more behind the familiar wheelbarrow. Every day I looked for an opportunity of carrying out my resolve, of which I had given no inkling to any. It was, however, some time before I considered my chances sufficiently good.

One afternoon, we, a group of thirty-two prisoners, were again working on the slopes outside the fort. We were cutting willows, and for this purpose it was necessary to enter the thick shrubbery. The moment I entered this shrubbery I looked around me and I made up my mind. In a moment I was over the moat, and set off at full speed. I was seen at once, and immediately all was in full cry behind me. Soon I noted ten of my pursuers close behind my back. Shot after shot was fired, the bullets whistled around me, but not one hit me. Thus I got to the open field, and would most certainly have escaped once more, had not God stepped before me in the way. Just at that moment a shepherd was returning home with his flock. He saw me with my pursuers at some distance behind me, and realised at once what was happening. "Hold him, Tiras!" he cried to his dog, and the beast sprang upon me in fury. In my terror I grasped the beast and tried to strangle it, but neither was I successful in this, and in the course of my struggle I was twice thrown upon the ground. Meanwhile the patrol had reached me, and once more I jumped up ready to fly. "Stand still!" they cried, "or we will shoot you through the head!" and with these words they surrounded me. But I was resolved upon freedom or death. I made a desperate leap and broke through the ranks of the search party once more. They stood amazed at my boldness and before they thought of shooting, I was already several hundred yards away. Three of them however raced after me; one on my left, one on my right, and one behind me. He on the left reached me first and struck me a blow on the forehead with his rifle, which dazed me. I recovered however and grasped him about the chest. Meanwhile, however, his comrade approached and fired at me. The bullet entered my left cheek and came out here at the back of my neck. I now lost consciousness. I was brought back as dead to the lazaret in Julich.

Shortly afterwards I came to again, but only to experience unspeakable pain. The surgeon cut out no less than seventeen larger and smaller pieces of bone from my neck and jaw. For three months I lay there without being able to speak a word or take anything other than a little thin soup. After this I lay in the lazaret for a further eleven months. Oh! gentlemen, that was a time which I shall never forget. The whole town knew about me, and the townspeople were permitted to bring me some small refreshment. I even received a visit on one occasion from three ladies. They were not able to produce much change in me, good though their intentions were. Would you ever believe it, gentlemen, that even now I remained just as hardened a sinner as before? When the ladies asked me whether I intended to make yet another attempt at escape, I replied without hesitation: "Yes, just as soon as I am restored to health."

14

And yet, however hard I appeared outwardly, within my heart something began to work which was not of the flesh. While I lay there in solitude, thought of what had happened in the past and cast a look into the future, the tears would often stream from my eyes. I felt that the hand of God was pressing heavily upon me, and frequently I said to myself: "Ah, you can get nowhere with your own strength. You have struggled for so long against God, and after all you have got no further than this miserable sick-bed and these oppressive bonds. How long will you fight against God? It would be better if you were to humble yourself under the mighty hand of God, and look for help from Him instead of from your own strength."

Thus I thought in my moments of sadness and despair, and then I would usually fold my hands in prayer, and there arose from my soul sighs which in truth were not heaved in vain. Many do not consider sufficiently, that God's work in spiritual things has very much in common with His work in nature. Everything takes place by means of a gradual development; there is much that goes on in secret below ground before the plant becomes visible above the surface. It may perhaps be thought that in the state at which I had now arrived, I was already converted from my wicked ways; and there are certainly not a few who would even then have congratulated me upon my conversion. But this would have been just as premature as when one should gather in a plant for harvest, because it shows some signs of life developing.

It has been my experience that conversion is preceded indeed by a great sense of sin and by many cries for salvation; but at the same time, that repentance itself is something other than a sense of sin and a cry for help. It is indeed much when a sick soul realises its malady and sends for the Physician; but with that alone he is not yet healed. He must also use the healing means, and not until these have worked within shall he find healing. It is true that when I sighed to God I was even then using the medicine which the great Physician prescribes so graciously to every *coming* sinner; for that is indeed a means of healing when a man comes to God, believing that He is, and that He is a rewarder of them that diligently seek Him. But not all coming to God is sufficient, and not all coming to God works at once a complete healing; here also there is a period of development necessary, and the spiritual medicines too require time to be able to work. In secret the malady then often rises to an even greater pitch than ever before, and those who have no knowledge of spiritual sickness and its healing, may then possibly assume that the patient was hopelessly lost. Many a serious thinking Christian would at least have passed this judgment upon me, had they seen me after my restoration from my sick bed.

For indeed, gentlemen, when I was discharged from the lazaret (a few days before my birthday), I left all my serious intentions and lamentations behind me on my bed. Now that I stepped once more into that miserable convict's life, I felt indeed very humbled but I sought comfort again in the flesh.

Although I was by no means enslaved to drink, yet I was a lover of this ruinous poison. In my prison, as you may well imagine, the opportunity did not often arise to regale. Now and again however, we succeeded in smuggling in a little gin or brandy; and, to their shame be it related, the officers of the fort itself sometimes gave their encouragement thereto.

Thus it was that I had managed a day or so before my birthday to come into possession of a considerable quantity of strong drink, and with my comrades I passed round the merry cup. Towards midnight we had emptied the whole bottle, and I was so giddy that I was swaying. The bunks in which we slept were built two or three above each other. I slept in an upper bunk so that in order to get into it, I had to use a stool. With great difficulty I managed to get upon the stool; but with the movement which I made to get thence into the bunk, I stumbled backwards and fell, my head grazing the iron coal hod, and with such force that even some of my hair remained stuck to its rim with blood. This sobered me at least for the moment to the extent that I could get into bed. But since I could not get to sleep, I heard a voice, which called to me: "This is the last time, if you ever drink again!" and that voice came like a thunderclap into my soul. I thought that it had clearly been an inward voice in my own heart; but to my great amazement I found the next morning that my comrades had also heard that voice. It is not my intention, gentlemen, to give my story a mist of the miraculous; I am prepared to believe them that this voice was perhaps that of one of the soldiers, particularly because there was in their number a devout man, with whom I later became acquainted.

But this I must say, that to me on that night this voice was as the voice of God from heaven, and it had such an immediate effect upon me that since that time I have never imbibed strong drink. The voice had not the same effect upon my comrades. While I spent the night in great distress they went peacefully to sleep. The next morning it was Sunday; and since they still had some strong liquor they wanted to tempt me again. I had however quite determined to take not a drop between my lips; and in order to escape their hands I made my way to a secret corner, where I remained until the church service began. I add this, gentlemen, merely to show that a man can indeed find a means of escape from temptation, when it concerns him in reality.

When we entered the church, the congregation was singing that hymn:

"Eternity, tremendous sound"
(i.e. "Eternity—oh thunder-word")

and my feelings were so touched that I could not refrain from weeping. "O my God!" I cried in silence, "What is happening to me; wilt Thou then not let me go? Must I then after all be conquered by Thee? Yes, if eternity is a thunder-word for any, then it is indeed to me!" During the whole service I was bathed in tears. I saw how often I had brought myself to the very verge of the eternal abyss and how God had, time and again, as it were, pulled me back from the jaws of hell.

When I came out of church, my comrades asked me tauntingly what was the matter with me. "Oh," said I, "leave me alone, I cannot tell you." I sought everywhere for quietness, but could find it nowhere; for I was continually surrounded by my comrades, and their teasing wicked language cut now through my soul. Under these circumstances Divine mercy was again put forth on my behalf; it pleased Him that I might find an opportunity of coming once more into solitude, there to pour out my heart before God.

Through my exertions and my fall the previous evening, the wound in my neck, which had not entirely healed, became worse. I was ordered by the doctor to return to the lazaret. There I spent some blessed hours—though the blessing was only revealed some considerable time later. For, gentlemen, and here you will certainly smite your hands together in amazement, with all my castings down and amid all my sighs and cries, I still would not give up the determination, as soon as an opportunity presented itself, of escaping . . .

15

One afternoon I picked up a Bible. I opened it first at the 34th Psalm. It was the ninth verse which particularly struck my eye: "Taste and see that the Lord is good." I laid the Bible down and sat deep in thought. But my train of thought was not as it should have been.

Instead of falling humbly at the manifold mercies which God had shown towards me, a sinner, in that He had yet spared my life and had given me time to repent, I began to murmur and even to blame my gracious Protector. "Taste and see that the Lord is good," said I to myself, repeating the words of Scripture, "But you have not experienced much of this goodness. What a lot you have had to go through, and all because you forgot yourself in a moment of temper! What fearful sufferings you went through in Spain! You had to go about almost naked and you were covered with vermin. Yes, God may be good to others, but He has not been so to you; He certainly has something against you which is no fault of yours!"—Thus I thought within myself, until once again I took up the Bible. There I read in the 37th Psalm, and the third verse: "So shalt thou dwell in the land, and verily thou shalt be fed." (Or as Luther's German Bible translation would appear to render it: "Remain in thy land and take care of thy sustenance in an upright manner").

This word was impressed upon my mind, and made room for better thoughts; though I had not yet reached a right attitude. "Remain in thy land" I repeated to myself, "that is something you have not done. You ran away in self-will and even now you are intending to escape again. Could this be the reason, perhaps, that God is chastising you? If only you had remained in your land, you might perhaps have received a free pardon from the king." But then again, "God," thought I, "has created this longing within me for freedom, and why then has He permitted me to be shut up within this dark dungeon while I am yet so young?" Thus my rebellious heart struggled continuously against God and His Word. There was a voice within me which repeatedly drove me to the Scriptures, and in a short time I began to spend my time in doing nothing other than reading those blessed pages. This was not entirely without effect. More and more I began to agree that what I found written there was perfectly true; but this one point I could not get over, that God was being hard with me. Oh, gentlemen! What patience Divine longsufferance had with me and what a cold, hard stone is the human heart, which can alone be softened by the power of God's grace!

It pleased God not to leave me to my own devices, but to grant me an interpreter who taught me better things. Among the soldiers who held watch over the lazaret, there was a Pole, by name Gottlieb Woykey, a man whom I shall never forget. He had observed that I read the Scriptures diligently, and this had moved him to seek an opportunity of having a talk with me.

"Baumfeller!" said he to me, "Do you still have a desire to escape?"

"Certainly! As soon as I possibly can."

"Don't do it, my friend! God has chastised you so much already, and why will you weary Him and enrage Him still further?"

"Rubbish!" I answered peevishly.

"But you really ought to consider whether now at last you should humble yourself under the mighty hand of God!"

"That is my business, it has nothing to do with you; it's easy for you to talk, for you are a free man; but if you were a prisoner like I am, you would have a different tale."

"But . . ."

"Not another word, I tell you; I don't need your chatter."

"Well, you are really cross with me, but I will come again tomorrow, do you hear?"

"There's no need to come, because I haven't invited you; I don't know why you should concern yourself about me."

The good fellow walked away in silence; but my heart throbbed within my chest while I was thus talking to him; for everything seemed to say within me: "You are wronging him; you are thrusting away the hand which God is stretching out towards you." But my proud heart would not admit it, and I made not the slightest effort to call him back.

The next morning, while I was walking in the courtyard of the lazaret, Woykey came to me again.

"From my room I can see into yours," said he. "I notice that you still read the Bible quite a lot. It seems that you are still a friend of it."

"Yes," I replied, "to pass away the time I do read it now and then."

"Well now, that's not a bad way of passing away the time. But do you not find the Bible something more than a pastime? I think I can see from your looks that you read that Word of God for another reason also. Now, is that not so?"

This question struck home deeply. He had hit the nail on the head; but I was ashamed to admit that he was right.

"Now," said he, as I stood before him in silence, "tell me, why do you read the Bible?"

At this repeated question I felt as though I might choke in his presence; for I realised indeed that tremendous things would take place within me, were I to pour out my heart to this man. I realised that he would take away from me all that I yet held fast with both hands of my pride; my conscience told me that it would be very easy for him to demonstrate that I was reading the Word of God in everything but the Spirit of God.

"Come," said I, "I've no time now. I am thirsty and I am going to get a jug of water."

With these words I bounded away from him; but that faithful heart was not to be discouraged. He stayed there and waited until I returned.

"Are you so angry with me then?" he asked, taking me kindly by the hand. "What have I done amiss that you should thus flee from me? Truly, I only intend your good; I love you, and God urges me to speak with you."

Ah! gentlemen! Any heart would have broken to hear the language of that dear child of God; and mine too threatened to break, but I stifled myself once more in my pride, and, biting my lips, I said, "You ask me why I read the Bible. But you tell me why you read therein."

"I? because it is like bread to my soul and medicine to my heart; the Word of my God which speaks peace to my soul. There I find true release from every dungeon and from all bonds. There I find my God and Father through Jesus Christ my Lord."

As he spoke these words it was as though a heavenly light shone from his eyes; but my eyes could not bear that lustre.

"Well," said I, tardily, "the Bible is not that to me. I cannot understand how I deserve to suffer so much. But I am not going to discuss it with you any further. Goodbye."

"Shall we exchange visits from time to time?" he called out after me.

"Just as you like," I replied dryly and without enthusiasm. How I must have offended that warm, loving heart with my ice-cold pride!

16

Meanwhile, coldly though I reacted against Woykey, there burned within my heart something which busied my thoughts of him day and night. I felt myself drawn to him; for my conscience told me that he was in the way of truth, and that it would be good for me to walk it too. Sometimes the thought arose within me: "Ah, perhaps he is a deceiver, who can talk very piously, but who is capable of betraying you and selling you short." Such thoughts, however, found no abiding place in my heart, and they disappeared completely when Woykey one morning brought me half of his ration of bread, and kept it up for six weeks. It was not indeed in this Prussian lazaret so scandalous as in the French one, but there was no likelihood of getting fat here either; a half portion of bread was a real boon which convinced me that Woykey loved me not only in word, but in deed. When he brought it on the first occasion, I was not willing to accept it; for though he, as a healthy soldier had a full ration daily (we, the patients, had but a third portion), yet I well knew that he had no more than enough. But though I refused to accept it, he insisted, and laid it upon my bed. This he did day after day, and thus we were often together; yes, as soon as there was a moment to snatch to be together, we let it not go by unused. By this means there arose in my heart a great love to this man; I felt that he was, as it were, bound into my heart. At length he had to leave the lazaret, having been posted to another part of the citadel. This was to me a heavy blow. I spent a day of sorrow when he took leave of me.

I received regularly, through a student-surgeon, little notes from him, in which sometimes a quantity of money was enclosed. Useful though that money was, yet I can assure you that the contents of the notes themselves were far more valuable to me; for they overflowed with love to the Lord and, for His sake, to me. He pointed out to me the Scriptures, admonishing me to walk in the right way by humbling myself before God and to seek salvation in Christ! Truly these little notes were like messages from heaven to me, like drops of dew upon a dry and thirsty land. I longed more and more to be possessed of the fear of the Lord, and I believed that even now I could deem myself a sinner called by grace.

What is there more cunning than the human heart? Who can fathom it? My religion was due more to the quiet solitude of the lazaret than to a true change in my heart. I was not aware of this, as long as I remained in the lazaret; but it became clear to me when once again I was discharged fit, and returned to the life of correction. Even so, the good seed which Woykey had sown in my heart in the lazaret, had sent forth roots incapable of extermination; I thought, though, that it had come to full growth, and this was a great mistake in my vain heart; for they were as yet but the young, tender grass shoots which peeped above the ground. I thought that I stood already like a rock immovably in Christ, and thinking thus, I considered it unnecessary to take heed lest I fell. It is a dangerous thing, gentlemen, when a man who has come to better thoughts, is secretly taken up and satisfied with his change of heart. True conversion is not quickly satisfied, but hungers continually for more righteousness. This has been made very clear to me in my own experience.

When I returned to the company of my fellow prisoners, I found myself suddenly within the cold, bleak fog of the sinful life. The swearing and blaspheming which assailed my ears, cut through my soul at first and made me keep silent. This silence was not for long unnoticed by my comrades and they began to mock me. "Ho, ho," said they, "surely you haven't turned Calvinist! Have you been in the third heaven? Do you think you can pray yourself out of the citadel? Come now, you pray for us then, and we will do some swearing to counteract it, and let's see who helps us first—God or the devil." At first I even took the trouble to reprimand them with words of Scripture; but that was like throwing pearls before swine. I therefore quickly gave up the practice, and continued to hold my peace, until at length they tired of mocking me. Meanwhile I sighed deeply under this awful way of life, and I began heartily to long to get out. Thus the spring of 1844 came round. The sun brought forth new young life in all creation. The birds filled the air with their songs of praise and spring wafted to me scents as it were of balsam, which seemed to come from a paradise. My heart opened up in yearning, and a powerful sense of the glory of freedom came upon me. "I *must,* I must get away from here!" re-echoed in my heart, and my resolve was taken to escape for the third time. Occasionally I met Woykey on the working guard and I did at least have the honesty to inform him of my resolve.

"Ah!", said he, "you always want to be stronger than God."

"But Gottlieb," I replied, "surely I am not wanting to escape from God? Shall I have in a foreign land a different God from now?"

"No, but God has not placed you in another land. Here you must remain, and if ever you do leave, it is God must bring you out and not you yourself."

"But God cannot be willing for me to remain in the fortress, amidst this life of wickedness."

"Baumfeller!" cried he, shaking his finger, "You are listening to something which an evil spirit is whispering in your ear. Listen rather to what God says. He giveth grace unto the humble!"

Woykey frequently spoke to me on this wise, and his words put me to shame; for I felt indeed that he was right. But in spite of all my struggling against my proud heart, the resolve to escape became stronger and stronger within me. And indeed, some courage was needed to conceive of such a plan, for I was under double guard of the garrison, and I was left hardly a moment alone. But what power is there, apart from God's which can bend the proud heart of man? On the 11th April at about 6 o'clock in the evening, on the way to the citadel, I met Woykey. "Tomorrow I am going to escape," I whispered to him. He was visibly moved by these words, and followed me to the citadel. There, in a corner of the room, he fell upon my neck and began to weep bitterly. He prayed me to forego my plan, but I remained unmoved in my resolve. And when at last he left me, I even called out after him: "Pray for me!"

I spent a sleepless night; I was in the throes of a great struggle. My conscience told me that I was doing wrong, but the thought of having to remain here in this frightful life, forced me with sheer irresistible force to a third attempt at escape. I did not pray; I was not willing to do so, for I felt in advance that in prayer I would lose my resolve to flee. Thus I spent the night by considering the various circumstances which would best suit my purpose, when we should be at work on the morrow, in bringing my escape to a successful conclusion.

17

The next day we had to work behind the bridgehead. This was a point highly favourable to my plan, for here one was at a distance from all fortifications. On this occasion I was at work with just one other convict and one guard. In the morning we worked from five until eight o'clock, when we had a half-hour pause for breakfast. My fellow prisoner threw himself down on the grass, while I started a conversation with the guard, whose name was Haruchek. After a few minutes the guard leaned back against a tree, and since I had broken off the conversation his eyes began to close. I wait a few minutes longer, until I see that he is asleep. With a pounding heart I sink down on one knee, gently remove his rifle from his arm and place it eight paces away amongst the thistles, and then, taking to my legs, I cry out to him recklessly from afar "Adieu, Haruchek."

While he awakes in fright and looks around in vain for his weapon, I hasten on at a furious pace until I reach the banks of the Roer. Here the two fort-fishermen were drawing in their nets. Seeing me, they rushed to grab me, but without hesitation I sprang into the river which at that point was at its broadest. I was a good swimmer and within a short while I reached the other side. At once, wet though I was, I ran on again, when some farmers, being aroused by the fishermen's shouts, made an attempt to catch me. Presently I turned back and leapt again into the river. Half swimming, half wading, I dropped ten minutes downstream, till I came to the great canal which leads from the bridge-head to the Roer. Here I almost drowned, but I managed to grasp some bushes and so got to the bank. Again I hurried on to the village of Aldenhoven. Here there were some more farmers at work, and in order to avoid them I went down a side track. But thus I fell right into the net. I had scarcely run twenty paces, when a border guard approached who recognised me and immediately arrested me. I made some resistance, but he called for the help of the farmers and together they brought me first to Aldenhoven, and when the gendarmes arrived from Julich I was again transported to the fortress. Soon afterwards I sat manacled in the detention room. The quartermaster ordered a watch to be held before my cell, and the first guardsman to take up this duty was . . . Woykey! Imagine my thoughts when I saw him. I shall not attempt, gentlemen, to describe the feelings which pressed my heart at that moment.

Two hours went by, and not a word was spoken by either of us. It was as though neither of us dared to be the first to break the silence. At last he stood before the grille which was within my cell door, and said: "I did pray for you —that they might capture you. So you see, I have a living God; for now you sit between four walls. It has come to pass precisely as I prayed it might."

I was silent; it was as though a thousand daggers pierced my heart. A mighty struggle assaulted my soul. All that was within me said that he was right, that I must humble myself before God, that I must acknowledge the almighty hand of God, which had turned my way upside down. But even now the hardness in my heart would not be softened. Therefore I was silent and spoke not a word!

At last Woykey was relieved, and now he asked me: "Can you pray?"

"No," said I, "not now." Then he went away. During the night he had to stand guard once more before the door.

"Are you awake?" he enquired, knocking upon the door.

"Ah, do you think I can sleep?"

"Good. I am here alone; no-one can overhear us; let us pray together."

Now he kneeled down before my cell door, and prayed with such warmth, such fervency, such urgency, that God would open my eyes; that—oh sirs, forgive me that I cannot here withhold my tears, for that night hovers unforgettably before my soul, and I can never think about it without shedding tears.

Here the recounter was silent for a time, while he gave vent to his tears. Neither could we conceal our emotions. In silence we sat down together; for us too this moment will never be forgotten.

Enough, continued our narrator, he prayed and wrestled as it were with God for the salvation of my soul, and ceased not till I cried: "God, be merciful to me, a sinner!"

Yes, I had to cry it at last, for my heart was threatening to burst. I could not resist so much love and mercy. I threw myself upon the ground and sprinkled the dust with my tears. "Yes," I cried aloud, "I am a sinner. Against Thee, Thee only have I sinned; be merciful unto me, O my God! Uphold me with Thy free Spirit!"

Woykey now stood up and cried: "Brother! Be of good courage. God is for you; in Christ all is washed away. His blood cleanseth from all sin. He saves sinners by grace." With these and many other words he spoke to me in tones of fervent love and joy. Broken was my heart, and into that broken heart there dropped down those words of everlasting comfort. I was reconciled to God through faith. A new life was begun in my soul.

For several more days I remained in my cell, and during that time Woykey visited me faithfully. They were sacred hours which we spent together. On account of my two previous escapes my sentence had been increased to thirty-one years; this was now changed to life imprisonment. With this sentence I was quite content, and desired now but to carry my chains to the honour of my God. But now, my heart having become at one with the will of God, and I being no longer willing even to consider escape, now it was God who put forth His hand for my release.

18

It was just at this time that General V.d.G. was appointed Commandant of the Julich citadel. He was a man who feared God. He had heard my history and visited me while I was still in the detention cell. I shall never forget how this man too spoke comfort to my soul. Oh, were all officers such children of God, how invincible would Prussia then be! He advised me to set down my life story in a brief letter and volunteered to forward it to His Majesty the king. Major B., also a sincere Christian took a great interest in my case. He provided me with paper and ink and assisted me in the compilation of the letter. The king's answer was gracious to the extent that my sentence was altered by ten years, so that I now had a term of forty-one years, and since I had requested to be moved from Julich to some other place, I was transported to Cologne.

In Cologne I had at first much to endure, in that especially my fellow-prisoners mocked me on account of my piety. It pleased God however, so to order affairs, that I was appointed to act as their schoolmaster, in order to instruct them in reading and writing between the hours of 5 and 7. This I did with great pleasure and enthusiasm; but this was the very cause of my pupils' enmity, for they preferred to spend this time in talking rather than in learning. In this way, I there became a stumbling stone to all my comrades. Even the Captains and non-commissioned officers hated me, and sometimes I would have my ears boxed with the words, "You Calvinistic dog! " I was given grace to bear all this in silence and to pray for them. At the same time there were some who were otherwise minded, who comforted my soul, and many Christians in Cologne bgan to be drawn to me in cords of love. The Earl of K., the divisional padre H., and other kind friends showed unto me the fellowship of love in Christ. I was sent food and gifts from all sides, so that I lacked nothing.

Thus I spent the best part of two years. I was truly happy and praised my God. At length I was urged to prepare an appeal to the king. The divisional padre H. added a few words of his own. To be brief, gentlemen, on the 15th July, 1846 answer was returned from Berlin that the matter would be investigated, and the officers of the citadel were to submit a report about me. This report had to come from the Captain who was at enmity with me and the testimony which he gave concerning me was so insipid, that it could only with difficulty bear the name. Now, however, the General intervened and demanded a new testimony. Grumbling the Captain obeyed this command; but looking at me maliciously he said: "You need not think you will be released, it will not help at all."

"O Captain! " I replied "It is God from whom I look for help; He can ordain matters so that I am free in four weeks."

"Well, we shall see," he cried, laughing.

The report was sent up on the 16th July; but now it was as though all hell was let loose. My comrades were furious with me. I was by no means sure of my life; and on one occasion, as I lay in my bunk at night, someone approached me in the darkness and stabbed at me with a knife, which however, did me not the slightest harm, for it passed between my arm and my side; it was clear that God had set His angels round about me. I still reckon it to be among the greatest wonders of my life, that I did not perish during this period. How often did I draw comfort from the 91st Psalm!

Four weeks later—yes precisely four weeks after the Captain had sent the report, the answer came back from Berlin.

Completely free! A king's pardon!

All my enemies were defeated. The Captain was sitting on his sofa when I brought him the document.

"I can't understand it," said he looking gloomily ahead.

But I rejoiced in God and so did all my friends with me. A citizen, who loved me, provided me with civilian clothes so that I could leave at once. Padre H. invited me to a meal. That evening there was a banquet in his home.

And now, gentlemen, my story is at an end. You know how I afterwards came back to my native town, and here in this city found work immediately. At present, by the side of my dear wife, I live as one saved from the dead, and ask only, how shall I glorify my God, who has been pleased to show me, an unworthy sinner, the long-suffering power and glory of that grace, which wearies not in saving the lost, and vanquishes enemies by love!

Note by the translator:

About three years ago, motoring back from Cologne towards Aachen, we noticed a signpost indicating the town of Julich. The name stirred memories and a short detour brought us to the centre of the town. Enquiries in improvised German led us to the discovery of what remained of the Citadel which features so much in the story. Well mellowed by time and covered for the most part with grass and shrubbery, the massive brick fortifications were still recognisable. We passed through the 'porterne', and found it was indeed a brick-vaulted tunnel, but serpentine—designed no doubt to prevent a straight line of fire into the Citadel. We entered the vast enclosure to find that builders were in occupation. All that remained of any original buildings appeared to have been demolished, apart from one facade which was being incorporated in a new school. The outer wall remained however, and we completed their circuit and enjoyed a picnic on their broad grassy top. We then decided to explore some of the passages, and magazines, or had they once been prison cells within the thickness of the ramparts? Before making our departure we were approached by a builder's foreman from whom we gathered that the structure was closed to the public owing to its danger. He was friendly, but conversation was difficult, and we left after a final glimpse at the ruined brickwork, which must have been 40 or 50 feet high at the rear where the ground falls away.

The experiences of our Fugitive have sometimes given food for thought. Would it be going too far to suggest that the Lord uses His providences sometimes as a prison-house, whence we would again and again escape by any possible means, were we left to ourselves. Disobedience certainly, but desertion also, may well be the cause of our 'imprisonment', and we would add sin to sin by attempting to escape? We may be sure there will be no satisfaction but only greater dangers, in joining a 'Foreign Legion'. What a mercy to be brought to the end of our proud rebellion, to see it as such, perhaps through the instrumentality of one of Zion's watchmen, but always through that of God's word, to be brought with our Prussian soldier to the same spot as the publican—'God be merciful to me a sinner'.